# The Peninsular Campaign And

# Its Antecedents

As Developed By The Report Of Maj.-Gen. Geo. B.
Mcclellan, And Other Published Documents

J. G. Barnard

**Alpha Editions**

This edition published in 2021

ISBN : 9789354508455

Design and Setting By
**Alpha Editions**
www.alphaedis.com
Email - info@alphaedis.com

THE

# PENINSULAR CAMPAIGN

AND

## ITS ANTECEDENTS,

AS DEVELOPED BY THE

### REPORT OF MAJ.-GEN. GEO. B. McCLELLAN,

AND OTHER

### PUBLISHED DOCUMENTS.

BY

J. G. BARNARD,

LIEUTENANT-COLONEL OF ENGINEERS AND BRIGADIER-GENERAL OF VOLUNTEERS, AND
CHIEF ENGINEER IN THE ARMY OF THE POTOMAC FROM ITS ORGANIZA-
TION TO THE CLOSE OF THE PENINSULAR CAMPAIGN.

NEW YORK:
D. VAN NOSTRAND, 192 BROADWAY.

1864.

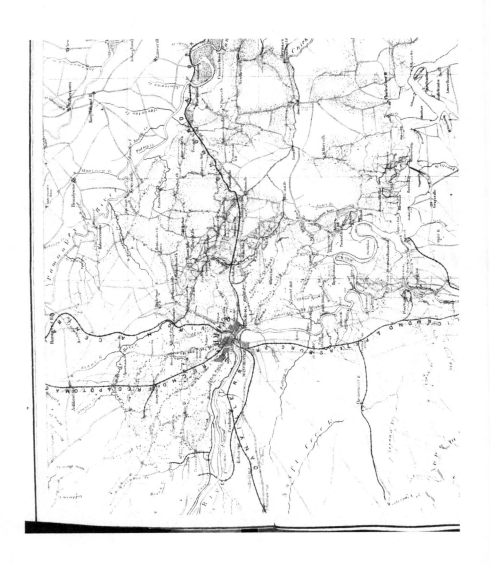

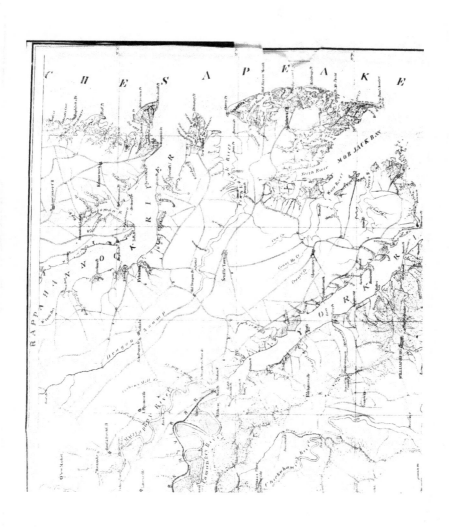

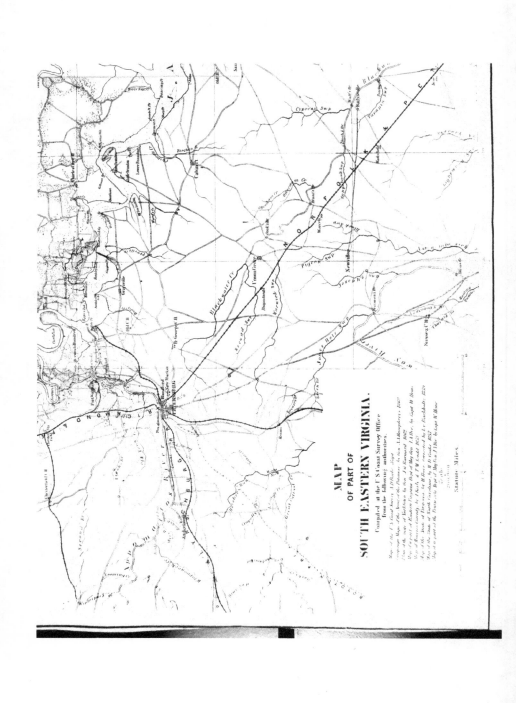

# MAP
## OF PART OF
# SOUTH EASTERN VIRGINIA.

Compiled at the U. S. Coast Survey Office
from the following authorities:

Map of the U. S. Coast Survey A. D. Bache...Asst.
Topograph. Maps of the Army of the Potomac...to 1862 A. Humphreys, Brig.
Plan of the route at Yorktown by Gen. J. G. Barnard, 1862.
Map of a part of Southern Virginia Dept. of May Gen. A. A. Dix, in Capt. H. Bear.
Map of Nansemond County by Church. of F. W. Lawble 1853
Map of the State of Virginia by H. Bear corrected by J. v. Fackhults, 1859
Map of the State of North Carolina by W. D. Cooke, 1857
Map of a part of the Peninsula Dep.t of May Gen. J. Dix by Capt. W. Bear.

Statute Miles

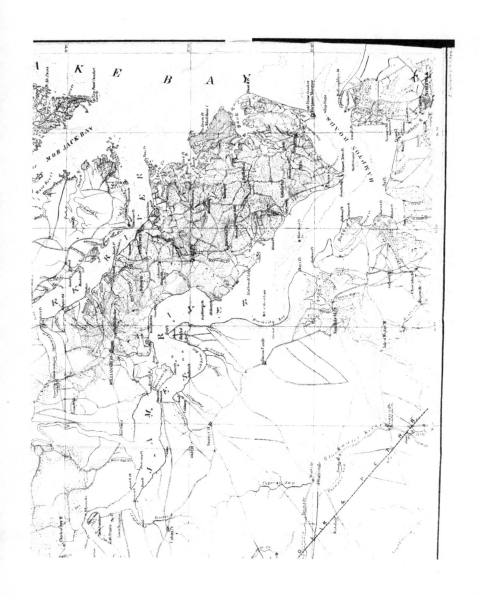

# PREFATORY REMARKS.

THE year of our Lord, 1863, opened upon the darkest period in the history of the momentous struggle in which we ... engaged. The Army of the Potomac, which had ...

## ERRATA.

Page 80, 5th line from top for 20th May read 20th June.
" 92, 17th " " " 20,000 " 200,000.

had but too faithfully followed the reverses of the East. The renewed hope which followed the repulse of the rebel armies from Maryland had been darkened by the long delays which ensued, and the subsequent disastrous failure at Fredericksburg.

Military calamities, disheartening as they might be, would have been of comparatively little moment, however, had military calamities been all that darkened the aspects of the time. The country was rich in men and means, and its resources had, as yet, been lightly drawn upon. It had put forth its strength, indeed, but not its whole strength. Men did not feel dismayed because they doubted the ability of the

STEREOTYPED BY
SMITH & McDOUGAL,
82 & 84 Beekman St., N. Y.

PRINTED BY
C. S. WESTCOTT & Co.,
79 John Street.

# PREFATORY REMARKS.

THE year of our Lord, 1863, opened upon the darkest period in the history of the momentous struggle in which we are yet engaged. The Army of the Potomac, which had gone forth in April of the previous year, at a period when victory had recently everywhere favored our banners and it seemed left only to give one vigorous blow to quell forever the rebellion, had been disastrously driven from Richmond, and called back to Washington, to arrive barely in time to save that city from the grasp of an enemy resuscitated in strength, and, with renewed audacity, assuming everywhere a vigorous offensive action. In the West the course of things had but too faithfully followed the reverses of the East. The renewed hope which followed the repulse of the rebel armies from Maryland had been darkened by the long delays which ensued, and the subsequent disastrous failure at Fredericksburg.

Military calamities, disheartening as they might be, would have been of comparatively little moment, however, had military calamities been all that darkened the aspects of the time. The country was rich in men and means, and its resources had, as yet, been lightly drawn upon. It had put forth its strength, indeed, but not its whole strength. Men did not feel dismayed because they doubted the ability of the nation to carry the struggle to a successful issue, but because, for the time, the power of the nation was partially paralyzed. Yet there never was a moment when the public safety, and the safety of the common cause more urgently demanded the exertion of all the nation's strength. Why, then, did men doubt? Where was the origin of this paralysis? It was in the charge, audaciously made, impudently persisted in, that to the blunders and incapacity of the Administration, all our disasters were due; that, with such incapacity at the head of affairs, our resources, though they were poured forth like water, would, like water, too, be spilt on the ground. Men will sacrifice much in great emergencies, but they never *will* give their lives or their money merely that such treasures may be ignorantly or wantonly wasted.

"Had McClellan but had *his* way, had *he* not been interfered with, had not his army been reduced and taken away from him, and his movements in a thousand ways hampered and balked, had he, in short, had the sole control of military affairs, all would have been different. Richmond would have been ours, the rebellion would have been subdued, and, instead of disaster and prolonged war, a triumphant peace might have been our happier lot." To such charges against the administration which had raised him to his position, and which, through the President, had ever showed him unwearied kindness, and given him all the confidence it *could* give, Gen. McClellan lent the full weight of his name and reputation. Throwing himself into the arms of a *party* bitterly hostile to that administration, associated with men who loaded the agents of the Government with reproach, and among whom were some so insensible to the honor of the country and the sacredness of the cause as to court foreign mediation and to meditate a disgraceful and humiliating peace, (1) to *him*, and to the erroneous ideas disseminated concerning *his* capacity, merits and agency, the paralysis of doubt was due, as it was to him were justly ascribable the disasters which brought our military affairs to so low an ebb.

The administration, thus denounced, was, for better or worse, the constituted agency through which the war, if it were to be carried on at all, *must* be conducted. *That* fact could not be altered. The men who weakened the arm of the nation's sole war-making power, just to that degree endangered the nation's cause. Therefore the question of Gen. McClellan's responsibility for our disasters ceased to be a mere abstract question about which men might differ without prejudice to the public interests; it became a national question, and one of vast import.

It was under such circumstances that, in writing an official report, at the request of Gen. McClellan himself, of the engineering operations of the Army of the Potomac, I deemed it my duty to state what I believed to be the sources of failure of the campaign of the Peninsula. The opinions therein written down were no afterthoughts. Six months before I had formed them, and when I spoke at all, (which i did not do openly,) *expressed them*. I had formed them painfully, reluctantly, at a period when political questions had not become involved with this subject, and no such causes existed to influence, in any manner, my judgment. It was at a period when for Gen. McClellan I entertained the warmest personal regard—a feeling which I distinctly and sincerely expressed in writing on leaving him in August, 1862. With no man have I ever, with a more absolute freedom from any other feeling than one of personal kindness, been so long closely associated, and if, at any moment, there seemed to me to exist some slight grounds for complaint, they were never such as to be remembered, or to have any abiding place in my breast.

But there are cases in which personal feelings must be allowed little weight. The destinies of nations cannot be trifled with, and in all that affects them, convictions of truth *must* be uttered. The Report of the engineering operations of the Army of the Potomac, and the statements of these pages, are the utterances I am constrained to make.

The review which follows was first prepared as a magazine article. It has not been thought necessary to alter the phraseology, though another form of publication is adopted.

J. G. B.

# THE PENINSULAR CAMPAIGN.

GEN. McCLELLAN had been called to the command of the Army of the Potomac with an unanimity of feeling and lavish bestowal of confidence, which stand almost alone in our history. The army looking upon Gen. Scott as past the age of further active service, and upon most of the officers of rank as superannuated or otherwise incapable of meeting such an emergency, hailed the advent of a new chief, whose juvenile promise, whose thorough military education, and whose already extended reputation, seemed to give assurance of precisely the one thing needed—a capable *leader*.

Under such circumstances, neither the nation, nor the administration, nor the army, were disposed to exercise—nor *did* they exercise—undue pressure. Every indulgence was extended to one upon whom so heavy a responsibility had been laid, for the acknowledged difficulties of the situation, and for his own inexperience and want of preparation.

Now, had Gen. McClellan been a Napoleon, with the prestige of a hundred victories—or even a Scott—old in the regard of the people—old in experience of war even upon a comparatively limited scale, but rejuvenated in years—had he been either of these—he might with propriety, if he thought the case demanded it, have drawn heavily upon the indulgence so freely extended. Being neither, it was important that he should make the lightest possible draft; that, at the very earliest moment, he should *do* something to confirm, continue and justify the nation's confidence. Of all Gen. McClellan's faults and incapacities, nothing—not even his irresolution and mismanagement in face of the enemy, nor his inability ever, in any case, to *act* when the time came—furnishes a clearer proof of the lack of those qualities which make a great general or a great statesman, than his failure to do this.

Let it be granted that it was not best to make any great movement till the winter of 1861–'62 had wholly passed away, (though there were the strongest political reasons against such delay,) yet Gen. McClellan should have been aware that, unless his prestige, through these long months, should be supported by *some* deeds, he would find himself virtually destitute of the power to carry out his own plans when the moment proper for such a movement should arrive; and so it happened. But, after six long months of omission, he added to his imprudence the positive folly of making an extravagant and senseless draft upon that confidence of the administration and the public, which in the beginning had been so generously given him, but which he had so lightly permitted to be, in a measure, lost.

Grant, again, that the lower Chesapeake *was* the true line of approach to Richmond, and the sole route by which to attain results of such magnitude as Gen. McClellan predicted from its adoption, yet, it was nevertheless true that this route was strongly disapproved by the President, and by many whose judgment carried great influence, and that it involved, in the minds of not a few, great danger to the Capital. Yet, in the face of all this, Gen. McClellan, who had never furnished any adequate evidence of his ability to plan or execute a great campaign, persisted in carrying off his army, at enormous expense, to a distant point, leaving that enemy, to whom he attributes a force of no less than one hundred and fifty thousand men, " well disciplined and under able leaders," confronting Washington, with nothing but the garrison of the place, and its very imperfect system of fortifications, to protect it. The line of forts on the Virginia side of the Potomac had been hastily thrown up, and was really, at that time, considering its great extent, very incomplete and weak; on the Maryland side it was so imperfect as hardly to deserve the name of a fortified line.

Gen. Barnard in his official report says, " When the army was to go by Annapolis, I felt confident that one-half would be no sooner embarked than the other would be ordered back to Washington." No one could, we think, have spent a week in Washington, at this period, without being convinced that, whether reasonably or not, such would have been the result of a mere demonstration of the enemy against the city. Congress was in session. Half its members already hostile to, and without confidence in, Gen. Mc-Clellan, looked upon his plan with distrust. In the event supposed, the citizens would have been frightened, and the President and Cabinet, alarmed and worried, *could* not have refrained from interfering to prevent the army from being withdrawn—more especially from being led away by one who had yet to establish his claim to such unlimited confidence in his military abilities.

Looking back to the middle of October, we find, by Gen. McClellan's own statement, that there were at that date 76,285 men under his command, disposable for an advance. There are yet before us three months of the finest weather, and the finest roads that were ever known in Virginia. It was of the *first* importance that Gen. McClellan should show himself possessed of a just claim to the nation's confidence ; it was of higher importance that foreign nations should not be allowed to see the rebellion swell, unchecked, until it should reach a stage which would justify their interposition.

Bear in mind, too, that at this very date, when he acknowledged himself to have a force, disposable for an advance, of 75,000 men, there commenced a series of events in the highest degree disreputable to the national cause—the blunder of Ball's Bluff *and the blockade of the Potomac*—and that for six weeks the enemy had flaunted his hateful banner in the very sight of the Capitol.

After rehearsing instructions given in November, as General-in-Chief, to various Commanding Generals, Gen. McClellan remarks, (p. 42,) " The plan indicated in the above letters comprehended in its scope the operations of all the armies of the Union, the Army of the Potomac as well. It was my intention, for reasons easy to be seen, that its various parts should be carried out simultaneously, or nearly so, and in coöperation along the whole line. If this plan was wise—and events have failed to prove that it was not—then it is unnecessary to defend any delay which would have enabled the Army of the Potomac to perform its share in the execution of the whole work."

We cannot regard this as other than an *afterthought;* and we think that the character of many other portions of the report, and its laboriously apologetic spirit, render this conclusion not uncharitable. There never was that concert of action, and never could be, between the forces in the different sections of the extended theatre of war, which would justify the Army of the Potomac in waiting a day for movements elsewhere. Moreover, the unnecessary inaction of the Army of the Potomac extends back, as we have shown, to a period prior to Gen. McClellan's assuming the functions of Commander-in-Chief.

In his apology to the President and exposition of his pet scheme of " changing his base" of operations to the lower Chesapeake, he says:

" When I was placed in command of the armies of the United States, I immediately turned my attention to the whole field of operations, regarding the Army of the Potomac as only one, while the most important, of the masses under my command.

" I confess that I did not then appreciate the total absence of a general plan which had before existed, nor did I know that utter disorganization and want of preparation pervaded the western armies.

" I took it for granted that they were nearly, if not quite, in condition to move towards the fulfilment of my plans. I acknowledge that I made a great mistake.

"I sent at once, with the approval of the executive, officers I considered competent, to command in Kentucky and Missouri. Their instructions looked to prompt movements. I soon found that the labor of creation and organization had to be performed there; transportation, arms, clothing, artillery, discipline, all were wanting. These things required time to procure them.

"The generals in command have done this work most creditably, but we are still delayed. I had hoped that a general advance could be made during the good weather of December; I was mistaken."

Take this in connection with the paragraph of page 42, just quoted, and we are bound to believe that no sooner did he reach the supreme command than he deliberately deferred all action of the Army of the Potomac, not because it was not *ready to act*, but until "a *general* advance could be made during the good weather of December." Without commenting upon the censure cast upon his illustrious and venerable predecessor, Gen. Scott, for the "total absence of a general plan, &c.," "the utter disorganization and want of preparation in the western armies, &c.," we remark that if the western armies were unprepared it was mainly because of his own insatiable demands for everything the nation could furnish, for all that he asked for was granted, as much as if he had been already commander-in-chief; moreover that, though he kept the Army of the Potomac spell-bound, waiting for "disorganized" and "unprepared" armies to move, those very armies actually *did move*, took Fort Henry, Fort Donelson, Columbus and Nashville, reached the very southern borders of Tennessee, and fought the battle of Shiloh before the Army of the Potomac had fairly inaugurated its campaign. Indeed, an admirer of Gen. McClellan's strategy of that day entered into a long newspaper argument to show why this great movement of the *right wing* must take place *before* the Army of the Potomac could be released from its compulsory inactivity.

Gen. McClellan cannot assign the mud obstacle, (hitherto so much insisted upon,) as an apology for inaction in a region selected by himself, and where, according to his own most formal statements, now published with his report, he believes that the roads *are passable at all seasons of the year*. Let us therefore accept his apology—he was *waiting* for the "combined" movements of other armies which *actually moved— effected great conquests and fought one desperate pitched battle*, before the campaign of his own Army of the Potomac was commenced!

But even if mud and the weather had been a cause for delaying the great movement in January, and February, and March, 1862, it was no reason that nothing should be done. The capture of Norfolk would have been a most important step, preliminary and accessory to a campaign against Richmond, with the James River, or, indeed, any part of the "lower Chesapeake" as a base. The failure to take that place during the winter virtually frustrated all Gen. McClellan's plans in this direction. The capture of this most important point would, if it had had none of the other results we have pointed out, have quieted the public mind, have given Gen. McClellan another lease on the rapidly waning public confidence, and have had an important bearing upon our European relations. The fitting up of the Merrimac as an iron clad ram was known to be going on at that period. Serious forebodings of the consequences which might ensue —forebodings afterwards too fully realized—were entertained by the Navy Department, by whom the capture of the place was urgently desired. Gen. McClellan alone seems to have been insensible to its importance. (2.)

A recent publication of Lieut.-Col. Lecomte, contains some matter of interest concerning this period of inaction, from October to March. The writer, a Swiss officer, who served as volunteer aid on Gen. McClellan's staff up to, and during a portion of, the siege of Yorktown, has translated into French the report of the Committee on the Conduct of the War, with notes and comments. These additions are thoroughly in the McClellan interest, defending his late chief against every charge, and lauding his generalship.

Col. Lecomte says the "secret service" of the army of the

Potomac was "particularly well" performed—that our information of the force and position of the enemy was very thorough—in fact that it was the special business of the *Orleans Princes*, (admirable young officers, doubtless, but not the best fitted, as foreigners, for the secret service duty,) and that on the 21st of February the "Count of Paris" presented Gen. McClellan with a statement of the enemy's force as follows:—

| | |
|---|---:|
| Division Holmes, (from Fredericksburg to Dumfries,) | 12,000 |
| Division Whiting, (from Dumfries to the Occoquan,) | 6,000 |
| A Division on the Occoquan, | 10,000 |
| A Brigade about Manassas, | 3,000 |
| Division Smith, between Manasses and Union Mills, | 17,000 |
| A Brigade of Cavalry at bridge over Bull Run, | 3,000 |
| A Division, (Longstreet,) at Centreville, | 14,000 |
| Brigade, (Hill,) at Leesburg, | 6,000 |
| Total, | 70,000 |
| And the "Division Jackson" at Winchester, | 12 to 18,000 |

Now Gen. McClellan states, in his Report, (p. 56, last par.,) that "from the Report of the Chief of the Secret Service," there were on the 8th of March at

| | |
|---|---:|
| Manasses, Centreville, Bull Run and Upper Occoquan, | 80,000 |
| Brooks' Station, Dumfries, Lower Occoquan, | 18,000 |
| Leesburg, | 4,500 |
| Total, | 102,500 |
| And in the Shenandoah Valley, | 13,000 |

A discrepancy of from 27,000 to 33,000 in the aggregate, and of 30,000 in the estimate of the rebel forces east of the Blue Ridge, and confronting Washington and the Potomac.

Col. Lecomte further states that, on visiting the rebel positions on the 11th of March, the Count of Paris had his map in hand, and found the accuracy of his estimates confirmed in a remarkable manner.* Now, the estimates so

* These estimates attribute to the enemy 70,000 men, from Fredericksburg to Leesburg—less than Gen. McClellan's "disposable force" of Oct. 15, 1861. Yet Gen. McClellan, at that early date, expressed officially his belief, founded

remarkably confirmed assign to Centreville, Bull Run and the Occoquan an aggregate of 47,000 men, whereas the report of the "Chief of the Secret Service," cited, assigns to the same region, *exclusive* of the "Lower" Occoquan, an aggregate of 80,000 men. The above statements and estimates may be properly left to Col. Lecomte and the "Chief of the Secret Service" to reconcile. They furnish evidence, however, of the real value of the "secret service" estimates as they are quoted in the "Report." Col. Lecomte's statement of numbers does not differ very much from one laid by Gen. McClellan before a council of war on the 2d of March.

It is next to certain that nothing like the numbers given even by the lowest estimate were in front of us, from Fredericksburg to Leesburg, at that time, and also that the evacuation commenced several weeks before the 8th of March. Wm. Henry Hurlbert, who certainly had most excellent opportunities of judging, and whose admiration of Gen. McClellan would not cause him to err consciously on the unfavorable side, says :—

"I have reason to believe that, when the history of the present war shall come to be written fairly and in full, it will be found that Gen. Johnston never intended to hold Manassas and Centreville against any serious attack; that his army at these points had suffered greatly during the autumn and winter of 1861–'2; that from October to March he never had an effective force of more than 40,000 under his orders; that his preparations for an evacuation were begun as early as October, 1861; and that after that time he lay there simply in observation."

Lecomte's remarks on the fortifications of Washington deserve special attention, considering the inspiration under which he writes. It has always been supposed that these fortifications, scarcely commenced when Gen. McClellan assumed the command, but renewed with immense energy

on reports of "spies, prisoners, &c.," that "the enemy had a force *on the Potomac* not less than 150,000 strong, well drilled, &c."[1]

from that moment—carried on under his own frequent inspection—were part of his great strategic plan; that they were to give security to Washington while he should move the bulk of his army even to a place like the Peninsula, where it could not possibly act directly in the defence of the Capital. It has been supposed, too, that the works constituting the defences of Washington, thus sanctioned and directed by Gen. McClellan, planned and executed by Gen. Barnard and his subordinates, emanating principally from one head and executed by one will, would form a system having unity and consistency, and in which we might find happy adaptations, and even high specimens of engineering skill. Col. Lecomte's account gives, however, quite a different view :—

"The construction was carried on under a feverish excitement; the soil was tormented, without truce or respite, throughout all the District of Columbia, and beyond."

"Every one ordered, in turn, a bit (*un bout*) of fortification, according to the needs of the moment, which fragment soon made necessary others in its connection; and so it continued, without having even yet ceased after more than two years. The result was a network of forts for which no person could be really responsible."

Another note-worthy remark of Lecomte. His low opinion of the fortifications of Washington does not permit him, consistently with his admiration for Gen. McClellan, to suppose that the latter had any confidence in them, and he is authority for the following design or idea on the part of his hero :—

"As to the place itself, (i. e., Washington,) to leave a portion of the works of the right bank (i. e., forts) outside of the real line of defence, and to *mine* them and *blow them up* under the enemy's feet. It was for this cause, doubtless, that the armaments of several forts had been neglected. This design, one may readily comprehend, could not be spoken of beforehand, nor exposed to indiscretions"!*

* So far from the "armament of several forts having been neglected," there was not a single fort in the line that had not been *heavily* armed. The only un-

The only REAL DEFENCE Washington had, then, was the Army of the Potomac, and that, as we know, was to be carried off to a region where by no possibility could it render aid, should the enemy, paying no attention to the safety of Richmond, choose to turn upon the capital. (3)

The movement by the lower Chesapeake having been determined upon, it was necessary to move the troops by water, and the President insisted upon the destruction of the enemy's batteries on the Potomac. Gen. McClellan admits the incredible fact that, under his authority, "preparations had been made for throwing Hooker's division across to carry them by assault." The barges (canal boats) were collected and fitted up, and the time of the expedition fixed. *A Ball's Bluff affair*, ten times intensified, would have been the certain result. Yet the assault *would have been made* but for "an adverse report from Brig.-Gen. J. G. Barnard." (See p. 50.) He adds that "a close examination of the enemy's works and their approaches, made after they were evacuated, showed that the decision was a wise one." And yet this project was deliberately gotten up as a preliminary to the embarkation of the army!

Just as the movement to the lower Chesapeake was about to be executed, the appearance of the long-expected Merrimac threw the whole scheme again into uncertainty. Now, though the "power" of the Monitor may have been "satisfactorily demonstrated" by the combat which occurred, it never was "satisfactorily demonstrated" that she could neutralize the Merrimac. It was all conjecture. All that the Secretary of the Navy, or Mr. Fox—all that Commodore Goldsborough—could affirm, was that she should not escape from Hampton Roads. The filling of Hampton Roads with transports, under such circumstances, was attended with great risk. The Prince de Joinville says: "These were the circumstances in which I arrived at Fortress Monroe. Soon the Roads were filled with vessels coming from Alexandria or Annapolis, and filled, some with soldiers, some with

armed or slightly armed works were those at Upton's Mill, which had special objects, and which it was never intended to arm permanently.

horses, cannon and munitions of all kinds. Sometimes I counted several hundred vessels at the anchorage, and among them twenty or twenty-five large steam transports waiting for their turn to come up to the quay and land the fifteen or twenty thousand men whom they brought. The reader may judge how fearful would have been the catastrophe had the Merrimac suddenly appeared among this swarm of ships, striking them one after another, and sending to the bottom these human hives with all their inmates! The Federal authorities, both naval and military, here underwent several days of the keenest anxiety. Every time that a smoke was seen above the trees which concealed the Elizabeth River, men's hearts beat fast. But the Merrimac never came. She allowed the landing to take place without opposition.

"Why did she do this?

"She did not come because her position at Norfolk, as a constant menace, secured without any risk two results of great importance. In the first place, she kept paralyzed in Hampton Roads the naval forces assembled to join the land army in the attack upon Yorktown; in the second place, and this was the principal object, she deprived the Federal army of all the advantages which the possession of the James would have secured to it in a campaign of which Richmond was the base."

Nothing, however, could divert Gen. McClellan from his movement "by the lower Chesapeake"—neither consideration for the President's convictions nor the dictates of ordinary prudence; but it is amusing that he should attribute the "retirement of the enemy" to his ascertaining that "the movement to the Peninsula *was intended*." Supposing the enemy to have had anything like the forces attributed to him, this theory supposes him to have been possessed with a stupidity inconceivable. Had he been timid as Gen. McClellan professes to believe, he would not have abandoned his strong and fortified "central position" until something more than rumors of an *intention* to embark our army should have reached him. He would have held his position till the movement had become *pronounced*. Had the enemy's "leaders" had, moreover, a small modicum of the "ability" which Gen. McClellan attributes to them, with an army of 115,000 men, they would not have retired even then. A serious menace upon Washington—to say nothing of a serious attack—would have frustrated the movement to the Peninsula.

The truth is, the enemy abandoned Manassas because his force was too weak, and because the risks were too great, to permit him to remain longer where he was. He abandoned Manassas after the President's *orders* for advance had been given—*a week after a council of war had been held to determine the means and modus operandi of attacking him where he was.* It is likely that he feared an "intention" of attack more than an intention of a "movement to the Peninsula," where he actually had a fortified line strong enough (*as it turned out*) to arrest our army a whole month.

Having with such affluence of argument demonstrated to the President the superiority of his "plan"—having tenaciously cherished it for four long months—having persisted, even against risks of no ordinary magnitude, and against the settled convictions of the President, in carrying it out, we cannot doubt that at least Gen. McClellan has perfect knowledge of the new theatre of war upon which he is entering—or, at least, such knowledge as would justify his assumptions and approve his military judgment. What, then, is our astonishment when we find that he carried his army into a region of which he was wholly ignorant—that the quasi information he had about it was all erroneous—that within twelve miles of the outposts of troops under his command a powerful defensive line had been thrown up during the winter and spring, of which he knew nothing whatever, though it lay across his meditated line of march, and altered the whole character of the problem—that the roads "passable at all seasons" were of the most horrible character, and the country a wilderness. His own account of his information is given as follows, (p. 74:)

"As to the force and position of the enemy, the information then in our possession was vague and untrustworthy.

Much of it was obtained from the staff officers of Gen. Wool, and was simply to the effect that Yorktown was surrounded by a continuous line of earthworks, with strong water batteries on the York River, and garrisoned by not less than 15,000 troops, under command of Gen. J. B. Magruder. Maps, which had been prepared by the topographical engineers under Gen. Wool's command, were furnished me, in which the Warwick River was represented as flowing parallel to, but not crossing, the road from Newport News to Williamsburg, making the so-called Mulberry Island a real island; and we had no information as to the true course of the Warwick *across* the Peninsula, nor of the formidable line of works which it covered."

*     *     *     *     *     *

And again, (p. 75 :) "In the commencement of the movement from Fort Monroe, serious difficulties were encountered, from the want of precise topographical information as to the country in advance. Correct local maps were not to be found, and the country, though known in its general features, we found to be inaccurately described in essential particulars in the only maps and geographical memoirs or papers to which access could be had. Erroneous courses to streams and roads were frequently given, and no dependence could be placed on the information thus derived. This difficulty has been found to exist with respect to most portions of the State of Virginia, through which my military operations have extended."

The censure thrown upon "Col. Cram" and "the topographical officers under Gen. Wool's command," is an ungenerous means of justifying himself. (4) It was for Gen. McClellan and his "secret service" to establish such investigations as would give him some light on the fundamental data of his campaign.

The withdrawal of the corps of Gen. McDowell from this expedition is the great incident upon which have been based the fiercest invectives against the administration for its "interference," and the charges upon it of responsibility for

the failure of the campaign. We shall go no further into
the matter, here, than to say, first, that the decision of the
corps commanders (pp. 59 and 60) and the approval of the
Secretary of War (p. 60) were the sole points of understanding between Gen. McClellan and the War Department.
Notwithstanding that Gen. McClellan was in the vicinity of
Washington eighteen days after those conditions were established, he never had, or took pains to have, an understanding as to how they were to be executed. (5.)    The
*very day* he sailed (April 1) he sent to the Adjutant-General
a statement of his dispositions, and this, submitted by the
Secretary of War to military advisers, and decided by them
to be *not* a fulfillment of the conditions, prompted and
justified the order withdrawing McDowell. With the Secretary of War and his advisers it was simply a question
whether the conditions which the President had imposed in approving, or rather in *permitting*, Gen. McClellan's eccentric
movement, had been fulfilled. They had *not* been fulfilled,
and the whole thing had been carried on from the beginning
in disregard, not only of the President's wishes, but of his
positive orders, and of the conditions which he (through a
council of war) imposed upon the movement. (6)

Citing the order detaining McDowell, Gen. McClellan re-
sorts to the unworthy subterfuge of representing it as a
*withdrawal of troops* from his command, by the President, in
violation of his promise " that nothing of that sort should be
repeated," (he refers to a previous withdrawal of Blenker's
division—a body of troops of which he had more than once
expressed his determination to rid himself in some way,)
" that I might rest assured that the campaign should proceed
with no further deductions from the force upon which its
operations had been planned ;" whereas it was simply an en-
forcement of the conditions upon which the President reluctantly sanctioned the plan.    He goes on to say :—

" To me the blow was most discouraging. It frustrated
all my plans for impending operations. It fell when I was
too deeply committed to withdraw. It left me incapable of
continuing operations which had been begun. It compelled

the adoption of another, a different and less effective plan of campaign. It made rapid and brilliant operations impossible. It was a fatal error."

The very circumstances he here details stultify his conclusions. "Rapid and brilliant operations" *were more than ever imposed upon him.* When Napoleon, with his handful of men, drove the Austrians out of Italy, though twice and thrice placed, by the paucity of his numbers, in almost desperate situations, it was not by admitting that "rapid and brilliant operations" were "impossible," (a word, by the by, which he ever repudiated,) but by recognizing that *in them alone* his hope lay.

The order referred to was received by Gen. McClellan simultaneously, almost (April 5th,) with the arrival of his army before the lines of Yorktown. As to the propriety of assaulting those lines, if there ever was a case in which such a step was not merely justifiable and advisable, but demanded by the circumstances, it was surely this. Through various causes not necessary to enumerate, the morale of the rebel forces was at its lowest ebb. That of our armies was high. Gen. McClellan, entering upon a campaign which he had obstinately inaugurated against the most earnest remonstrances of the President, found himself interrupted by an obstacle wholly unknown to him, proving, at the same time, the utter defectiveness of his data, and his own culpable negligence in failing to obtain proper information upon which to base a campaign. He had trifled with the destinies of the nation in thus, with more than childish levity and obstinacy, leading its most powerful army into such a situation. There was but one way to get out of the scrape—to break down the obstacle by a vigorous assault. Again, he was entering upon his virgin campaign as commander of a great army. Had there been no antecedents it would have become him to inaugurate this campaign and his career by a *coup de vigueur* which should carry terror to his enemies, and firmly fix himself in the estimation of his troops. But there *were* antecedents. Eight months of inactivity had shaken his reputation with the President and with his own nearest friends, while it had destroyed confidence in the minds of the majority of the most influential of his countrymen. The attack of Napoleon on the bridge of Lodi was certainly the very sublimity of rashness; he made it with nice apprehension of the relative *morale* of his own troops and of that of the Austrians, and of the effects of an action of such extraordinary boldness. Though not to the same degree, perhaps, there *was* a corresponding difference in the morale of the Union and rebel armies, and the most powerful motives for a corresponding boldness of action. All chances of success of the campaign turned upon not being delayed at Yorktown.

We believe that there must be some error in the assertion that Gen. Barnard "expressed the judgment that these works could not, with any reasonable degree of certainty, be carried by assault." Gen. Barnard pointed out where the lines were weak, and, without recommending one thing or the other, expressed the opinion that *if he could depend upon his troops*, he would assault there. It was for Gen. McClellan, who knew his troops better than Gen. Barnard, (the latter's duties not bringing him into close connection with them,) and who was solely responsible, to decide the matter.

The description of the works extracted from Gen. Barnard's report, (p. 84,) to the Chief Engineer U. S. A., *gives their condition as it was May 5th*, one month after we first encountered them, and after the whole force of Johnston had been working during all that time upon them; the process of throwing up earth works, mounting guns, forming embrasures, &c., having been going on day by day, under our observation, for the whole period. When we first saw them, (April 5th,) there were very few guns upon them, and those mostly field or siege guns on travelling carriages, in barbette, and which could not have maintained their positions against a vigorous cannonade. The connection between Fort Magruder and the "red redoubt" was a mere rifle pit, and from the "red redoubt" to the swamp *there was nothing whatever*.

The ground between and behind these two works was seen and could be swept by our artillery fire. Our assaulting columns would have been from two-thirds of a mile to one mile removed from the artillery of Yorktown, from the fire of which undulations of the ground afforded much cover, even supposing that the fire of that place could not have been subdued by our own batteries. The "red redoubt" towards which the assault would have been directed was a very insignificant work.

When Gen. Grant arrived before Vicksburg he thought it necessary to try the efficacy of an assault. In so doing he, at least, satisfied his army and satisfied the public mind. All the motives which could justify Gen. Grant existed in the case before us, intensified by the circumstances we have already noticed. (7)

We shall not pause here to dwell upon the battle of Williamsburg. That a fierce battle was fought at a point where there was a strong probability that such a rencontre would occur, (for it was reasonable to suppose that the enemy would require further time to secure his retreat and save his trains, and here was a fortified position perfectly adapted to such a temporary stand,*) that it occurred without foresight, preparation or orders, and that there was utter confusion with regard to the command and direction of the troops, that the Commanding General himself, though only 12 miles distant, was "completing the *preparations* for the departure of Gen. Franklin's troops by water, *and* making the necessary arrangements with the naval commander for his co-operation," that we lost 2288 men in an affair in which we gained nothing and which need not have cost us a man, is all now well understood.

Neither shall we dwell on the extraordinary sluggishness of the march from Williamsburg to the Chickahominy, following the Commanding General's boastful declaration that he should "push the enemy to the wall." (A dispatch, by the by, which he has suppressed in this report.) We shall only stop to call attention to the dispatch of the Secretary of War of May 18th, (p. 96,) and to the following comment of Gen. McClellan: "It will be observed that this order

* "It was also known that there were strong defensive works at or near Williamsburgh," (McClellan's Report, p. 74.)

rendered it impossible for me to use the James River as a line of operations, and forced me to establish our depots on the Pamunkey, and to approach Richmond from the north.

" I had advised and preferred that reinforcements should be sent by water, for the reasons that their arrival would be more safe and certain, and that I would be left free to rest the army on the James River whenever the navigation of that stream should be opened.

" The land movement obliged me to expose my right in order to secure the junction, and as the order for Gen. Mc-Dowell's march was soon countermanded, I incurred great risk, of which the enemy finally took advantage, and frustrated the plan of the campaign."

We here remark that it was at *Roper's Church*, where the army was on the 11th of May, that it was necessary to decide whether we would cross the Chickahominy near that place and approach the James (then open to us by the destruction of the Merrimac) or continue on the Williamsburg road to Richmond. The great mistake of not taking the James River route was made eight days previous to the date of this order, and was due to Gen. McClellan's total ignorance of the topography of the country he was operating in, to his want of any due appreciation of the superior value of the James as a base, and *not* to an order received eight days later.

In his eagerness to make this grave charge against the War Department, and to manufacture excuses for his own oversight, (to use a very mild term,) he has forgotten his own evidence, given under oath, before the Committee on the Conduct of the War, as follows :—

" *Question.*—Could not the advance on Richmond to Williamsburg have been made with better prospect of success by the James River than by the route pursued, and what were the reasons for taking the route adopted ?"

" *Answer.*—I do not think that the navy at that time was in a condition to make the line of the James River perfectly sure for our supplies. The line of the Pamunkey offered greater advantages in that respect. The place was in a better position to effect a junction with any troops that might move from Washington on the Fredericksburgh line. I remember that the idea of moving on the James River was seriously discussed at that time. But the conclusion was arrived at that, under the circumstances then existing, the route actually followed was the best. I think the Merrimac was destroyed while we were at Williamsburg." (8)

Next to the taking away of McDowell's corps the most important specification against the administration for interference, has been founded upon the compelling of Gen. McClellan to base himself upon the York and Pamunkey Rivers, instead of the James, in order to connect with McDowell, and Gen. McClellan himself does not scruple to assert it, though, in so doing, he contradicts himself. The stamp of disingenuous afterthought—so palpable on every page of the report to those who are familiar with the march of events of this campaign—is here made palpable to the general reader.

On the 18th of May our depot was firmly established on the York River. The army was well nigh up to the Chickahominy, the right wing on the New Bridge road, the left wing on the Bottom's Bridge road.

Gen. Barnard has given in his report a concise description of that (now) well-known stream, calling it "one of the most formidable military obstacles that could be opposed to the advance of an army; an obstacle to which an ordinary river though it be of considerable magnitude, is comparatively slight." Formidable as it was, Gen. B. further remarks, "the barrier of the Chickahominy being left unguarded at Bottom's Bridge, no time should have been lost in making use of the circumstance to turn and seize the passage of New Bridge, which might have been done by the 28th, and even earlier, had measures been pressed for taking it."

In reference *to the same period* and the same obstacle we find in the report before us, (p. 100, 1st par.,) "In view of the peculiar character of the Chickahominy, and the liability of its bottom land to sudden inundation, it became necessary to construct between Bottom's Bridge and Mechanicsville, eleven (11) new bridges, all long and difficult, with extensive log-way approaches."

It may here be remarked that we knew as little of the "peculiar character of the Chickahominy" and "the liability of its bottom land to sudden inundations" as we confessedly did of the topography and roads and physical character of this whole region—nothing at all.

The "eleven new bridges," (including in this enumeration the railroad bridge, Bottom's Bridge and New Bridge,) are here emphatically mentioned as if *at that date*, (May 24th,) it was as "necessary to construct" all these, as if the construction of each and all had been part of the programme, preliminary to any further motion. If this is not asserted, the idea is conveyed by the 1st par., p. 100, and confirmed by the 8th and 9th. ("The work upon *the bridges* was commenced at once," &c., &c.)

By reference to Gen. Barnard's report, (p. 21,) it will be seen that, at this period, *three* points for bridges were selected in front of the right wing of the army near "New Bridge," viz.: one, a half mile above, another, the same distance below the "New Bridge," and the New Bridge itself. The latter was the crossing of the turnpike, and required no more than an hour or two of work in throwing a pontoon bridge, *when the time of crossing should come.* The other two required corduroy work, which could not be done at all, (at least it was not part of the plan to do it,) until the *same moment should arrive.* All that could be done is stated in Gen. Barnard's Report, viz.: to " collect the bridge materials and corduroy stuff;" nor was any very extensive work anticipated, as the bottom lands were quite dry, and no inundation had yet occurred or was anticipated. Gen. McClellan was not waiting for the bridges, but the bridges were waiting for Gen. McClellan. At Bottom's Bridge, (one of the " eleven,") *two* new bridges *had been completed*, approaches and all, on the 23d, (May.) On the 27th the railroad bridge was completely repaired.

Intermediate between Bottom's Bridge and the three points mentioned by Gen. Barnard, (where alone a passage was to be forced,) Gen. Sumner had built two bridges with long corduroy approaches through the swamp; they *were both finished* about the 28th. There was no enemy to oppose their construction.

Gen. Barnard says, "So far as engineering operations were concerned, the whole army could have been thrown over as early as the 28th." And such an operation was daily looked for in the army, and was the avowed intention of Gen. McClellan.

But, (between Gen. McClellan's plans and their execution there is *always* a " but,") " a considerable force on his right flank " caused him to delay and to send off Porter to achieve his "glorious victories" which so puzzled the President, and of which he is so unable to " appreciate the magnitude."

This really useless expedition was undertaken just at the moment when Gen. McClellan was " ready," (if he *ever* was ready,) to force the passage of the Chickahominy. The last few days of comparatively dry ground, favorable for the execution of this operation, were thus lost. On the 30th the tremendous rain storm set in which inundated the swamp and bottom lands. On the 31st the enemy attacked our isolated left wing. Had he delayed that attack twenty-four hours it would have been fatal to that wing, and put a disastrous period to the campaign; for Sumner could not have crossed, and the two corps assailed would have been crushed without his aid. Man cannot control the elements, indeed, and man, perhaps, could not foresee this inundation; but *every* delay, in military affairs, is a *risk*, and such proved to be the risks which this needless delay involved—a delay voluntarily incurred in a false and dangerous position.

The promptness of Sumner, and the intelligent foresight he displayed, enabled him to reach the field, and to turn defeat into victory. His columns were formed and their heads pushed up to the bridges, that, when the expected order should come, he might be at once in motion. Thereafter the battles which ensued took the usual course. Gen. Sumner, the highest officer of the army next to Gen. McClellan, arrived late in the day, with a part of his corps, to meet the enemy on ground he had never seen—to aid another body of troops the positions of which he knew nothing of. Rightfully, after his arrival, he commanded on the battle-field, but neither he nor Gen. Heintzelman encountered each other, nor could act with intelligent reference to each other's position. No supreme head, knowing the whole ground, gave unity to action or coherence to the masses. On the second day, indeed, Gen. McClellan, when the serious work of the day was ended, made his appearance. (9)

The enemy being finally repulsed, at an early hour on Sunday, (June 1st,) the "only available means" of uniting our forces at Fair Oaks for an advance on Richmond, and thus to obtain some results from our victory, was *not* to march them twenty-three miles, as described p. 112, (a con-siderable exaggeration of the necessary average march of the army by the route described,) but to move a force from Sum-ner's command to take possession of the heights near Gar-nett's and Mrs. Price's houses, and *then* to bring over our right wing by the New Bridge, (actually made and passable for troops and artillery at 8.15 A. M. on the morning of June 1st.) A single division could have cleared those heights.

Gen. McClellan states, (p. 113:) "In short, the idea of uniting the two wings of the army in time to make a vig-orous pursuit of the enemy, with the prospect of overtaking him before he reached Richmond, only five miles dis-tant from the field of battle, is simply absurd, and was, I presume, never for a moment seriously entertained by any one connected with the Army of the Potomac." (9½)

An ingenious evasion of the real point at issue. It was not to "overtake the enemy before he reached Richmond," but to *follow him up into Richmond*, that constituted a "taking advantage" of the victory of "Fair Oaks." That we might have entered Richmond, all the information since obtained goes to prove. Wm. Henry Hurlbert says: "The roads into Richmond were literally crowded with stragglers, some throwing away their guns, some breaking them on the trees—all with the same story, that their regiments had been 'cut to pieces;' that the 'Yankees were swarming on the Chickahominy like bees,' and 'fighting like devils.' In two days of the succeeding week the provost-marshal's guards collected between 4,000 and 5,000 stragglers and sent them into camp. What had become of the command no one knew."

Gen. Heintzelman states that, " after the enemy retired, he gave orders to pursue them;" that he " countermanded" the order on Sunday, in consequence of Gen. Kearney's suggestion and allegation that " Gen. McClellan would order a general advance in two or three days." The next morning, on learning that the enemy had fallen back in great confusion, he sent his troops "forward, and they got within about four miles of Richmond;" but, on sending word of it to Gen. McClellan, he was ordered to "stop and fall back to the old lines."

Gen. Sumner testifies: "If we had attacked with our whole force, we should have swept everything before us;" and "I think the majority of the officers who were there think so now."

Gen. Keyes testifies: "After the battle of Seven Pines there was another time when I think, if the army had pressed on after the enemy with great vigor, we should have gone to Richmond; and, in connection with this last, I am compelled to state that I think Gen. McClellan does not excel in that quality which enables him to know when to spring."

We have, thus positively, the opinions of the commanders of the three corps engaged in the battle.

The Prince de Joinville says: "Some persons thought, *and think still*, that if, instead of Sumner alone, all the divisions of the right wing had been ordered to cross the river, the order would have been executed. It is easy to see what must have happened if, instead of 15,000, 50,000 men had been thrown upon Johnston's flank. But Sumner's bridge, no doubt, would not have sufficed for the passage of such a force. At midnight the rear of his column was still struggling slowly to cross this rude structure, against all the diffi-

culties of a roadway formed of trunks, which slipped and
rolled under the horses' feet, of a muddy morass at either
end, and of a pitchy dark night rendered darker still by the
density of the forest. But several other bridges were ready
to be thrown across at other points. Not a moment should
have been lost in fixing them, and no regard should have
been paid to the efforts of the enemy to prevent this from
being done. *Johnston had paraded a brigade ostentatiously,
as a sort of scarecrow, at the points which were most fitting
for this enterprise ; but the stake was so vast, the result to be
sought after so important, the occasion so unexpected and so
favorable for striking a decisive blow, that in our judgment
nothing should have prevented the army from attempting
this operation at every risk.* Here again it paid the penalty
of that American tardiness which is more marked in the
character of the army than in that of its leader. It was not
till seven in the evening that the resolution was taken of
throwing over all the bridges, and passing the whole army
over by daybreak to the right bank. It was too late !"

The Prince here labors under that excusable confusion of
ideas which arises from an amiable unwillingness to carry
his own convictions to a logical conclusion. "It was not till
seven in the evening *that the resolution was taken,*" &c.
Now, the army had been waiting for several days for that
"resolution" to be taken. The moment it *was* taken the
bridge building commenced. The rising flood and the darkness of the night interfered with any progress till daylight
dawned; but at eight o'clock the next morning one bridge
was finished, and the passage practicable *for all arms;*
during the day two other passages became practicable for
*infantry.* So far from being too late, the bridges were
ready just in time.

The Prince further says: "What might not have happened, if at this moment the 35,000 fresh troops on the
other bank of the Chickahominy could have appeared upon
the flank of this disordered army, after passing the bridges
in safety !"

Gen. Barnard states (p. 23 of his "Report") that " at 8.15

A. M. (June 1st) the pontoon bridge at the site of New Bridge was complete and practicable for infantry, cavalry and artillery. About noon the 'upper trestle bridge' was practicable for infantry. It was not till night that a practicable bridge for infantry was obtained at the 'lower trestle bridge.' " He adds that, owing to the overflowed condition of the bottom lands, the two last bridges could not be made practicable for " *cavalry or artillery*" without extensive corduroying. He further remarks: " There was one way, however, to unite the army on the other side; it was to take advantage of a victory at Fair Oaks, to sweep at once the enemy from his position opposite New Bridge, and simultaneously to bring over, by the New Bridge," (with which, we remark, a raised turnpike communicated,) " our troops of the right wing, which could then have met with little or no resistance."

" Our first bridges carried off or rendered impassable," (alluded to p. 100,) were the two bridges made by Gen. Sumner, which were too remote to have ever been counted on for the close connection of the parts of the army. *No bridges*, thus designed or commenced, were ever carried away, *for none were commenced before the flood occurred.* Bottom's Bridge, it is true, became " impassable," but this was never counted on for movements of troops, being too remote. The railroad bridge continued passable, and supplied our army, and by its means also infantry, in unlimited numbers, could pass.

The true statement of the case is, that the favorable time for forcing a passage at the " New Bridge" (by far the best crossing of the Chickahominy, and one which no inundation could seriously impair,) having been trifled away, as has been already shown, and the opportunity of seizing this passage which the battle of Fair Oaks offered having been lost, *then* the heavy labors of bridge building commenced, and the inundated condition of the swamp necessitated the laborious and extensive structures called " Woodbury and Alexander's" and " Duane's" bridges, besides two or three foot bridges, which required little labor. Then, too, in prosecuting the "upper" and "lower trestle bridge" corduroys, "our men were exposed to the enemy's fire," and as it is impossible to lay heavy corduroy roads under fire, they were abandoned and never became available.

We have passed through one crisis, and have shown that it was *invited* by the dispositions of Gen. McClellan, by which our army was permitted to be for a whole week divided into two distinct portions, entirely isolated. (10) This arrangement took place at a moment when Gen. McClellan avows his belief that the enemy's numbers "greatly exceed our own," and that he has every reason to expect desperate work. (p. 98.) The weaker of the two isolated portions was thrust forward to within seven miles of Richmond, with no obstacle whatever between it and the enemy's superior forces, on ground that had *no* natural strength, and to which little artificial strength could be given, under the circumstances. The position, too, in which our troops were thus risked was never seen by the commanding General until after the battle of Fair Oaks.

The weakness of the enemy, combined with his blunders, alone saved us. Gen. McClellan did not believe in his weakness—he had no right to count on his blunders. *Such* is the generalship which can do nothing "rapid or brilliant," owing to alleged numerical weakness, but which, in delay, hesitation and uncertainty, incurs risks such as the rashest of daring and energetic generals seldom encounter. (11)

The failure of the enemy to crush our left wing, though he unquestionably exerted his whole strength to do it, might well shake Gen. McClellan's credulity with regard to his "superior numbers," and authorize his otherwise illogical statement (see telegram, June 7th, p. 115) that he should be "*in perfect readiness*" to move forward and "*take Richmond* the moment McCall reaches here and the ground will admit the passage of artillery." With "superior numbers" of the enemy and "strong works" around Richmond, it is astonishing with what facility he is always "taking Richmond"—*in his dispatches!*

Again, (June 10th,) though he has information that

"Beauregard has arrived," and "some of his troops are to follow him," he announces, "I shall attack as soon as the weather and ground will permit;" and he reiterates in the same dispatch, lest he should not be understood or believed, "I wish to be distinctly understood that whenever the weather permits, I will attack with whatever force I may have," &c. (p. 116.)

McCall arrived on the 12th and 13th. The rains of the early part of the month slackened as the month advanced, so that on the 14th the General announces "weather now very favorable." The ground grew firmer as the June sun continued to act upon it, and by the 20th artillery could operate with facility. On this date the General telegraphs that he has "no doubt Jackson has been reinforced from here." Now, then, is the time to "move forward" and to "take Richmond." But, instead of "perfect readiness," we hear the "difficulties of the country" expatiated upon—we learn that "by to-morrow night" certain defensive works will be finished—that the construction of these "defensive works" is rendered necessary by his "inferiority of numbers," so that he can bring the "greatest possible numbers into action," &c., &c. Instead of "*attacking with whatever force he has*"—instead of "perfect readiness" to act, (though he learns the enemy has been reduced by detachments,) he is waiting for "defensive works;" and, instead of "taking Richmond," or doing anything towards it, he "would be glad to have permission to lay before the President, by letter or telegraph, his views as to the *present state of military affairs throughout the whole country*"!

Bear in mind that, two months before, Gen. McClellan had been relieved from a position which made the expression of such views a part of his official duty; and now, *after* having been so relieved, at *such* a moment as this, when the President is eagerly scanning each telegram to know if the army has really "advanced" and "taken Richmond," he is astounded to find only an offer of "views" on the "present state of military affairs throughout the whole country," coupled with a modest request to know "the numbers and positions of the troops not under his command in Virginia or elsewhere." In other words, Gen. McClellan, at a moment so critical to himself, and under circumstances which should concentrate all his thoughts upon the work immeately in hand, asks to be informed of the numbers and positions of all the troops of the United States!

So neither McCall's arrival nor fine weather constituted "perfect readiness to advance." All the "eleven" bridges are finished—even the "defensive works" will be ready "by to-morrow night (viz., June 21st)—and yet he does not "move forward."

Here is something, at least, that ought to start him. Thus far "all the information previous to June 24th," &c., (p. 119) induced the belief that Jackson was at Gordonsville, receiving reinforcements *from* Richmond. *Now* (June 24th) Gen. McClellan learns that Jackson was moving to Fredericshall with his own troops and all those "reinforcements" that had gone to him, for the purpose of "attacking my rear on the 28th."

Surely now is the time, if ever, to "move forward;" in two or three days the enemy will receive heavy re-inforcements. So, at last, on the 25th, our bridges and intrenchments being "at last completed," (N. B. The bridges were all completed by the 19th, the "defensive works" were announced June 20th, as to be completed to-morrow night," viz., June 21st, and, we remark, they were ready enough *at any time* for an advance,) *something* is really to be done. The reader holds his breath to know what is to follow—it is, "*an advance of our picket lines of the left* PREPARATORY to a general forward movement." One would think that the art of "preparation" had been exhausted, but if so simple as to believe that the time for *preparing* to do a thing ever ends, and the time of executing it ever commences, his military education could not have been acquired under Maj.-Gen. McClellan. *This* preparatory operation at any rate must be the *last*. But alas! though "successful in what we have undertaken," the courage which, in the morning was screwed up to order "an advance of our picket line of the left, preparatory to a general forward movement," has all oozed out by " 6.15 P. M." "Several contrabands," (we hope they were intelligent ! !) "just in," announce that " Jackson's advance is at or near Hanover C. II. ;" that the perpetual bugbear, Beauregard, "had arrived," and that the rebel " force is stated at 200,000 men, including *Jackson* and Beauregard."*

The "general forward movement" of the morning is totally forgotten after the interview with these " contrabands," and we have this feeble announcement : " But this army will do all in the power of men to hold *their position and repulse any attack*." Regretting his "inferiority of numbers," for which he is not " responsible," he " will do all that he can do with the splendid army he has the honor to command," (Oh, that in such a moment surely every reader will aspirate such an army *had but a leader*,) and if destroyed by "overwhelming numbers " " can at least die with it and share its fate." *For once*, however, he feels that " there is no use in *again* asking for reinforcements."

Thus in the morning we are treated with a grand "preparatory movement," (what the particular necessity of losing a whole day, when time was so precious, in this absurd manner, the uninitiated can scarcely comprehend,) for a " general advance," and by sunset we have this feeble wail of despair. Does any one believe that any such sudden and portentous change had come over the state of affairs, as would justify such a change in the spirit of the General, or that the tales of "several contrabands " could so completely turn the tables ? If he does not believe this, then the alternative is to believe the Report which contains such statements to be a mere veil—transparently thin—with painful labor, drawn over the writer's conscious ignorance of his own plans, intentions or situation.

He goes on to say, (p. 122,) "on the 26th, the day upon which *I had decided as the time of our final advance*," (it

---

* As early as June 10th the General has "information that Beauregard had arrived," and " that some of his troops were to follow him." The "contrabands" bring no *news* after all. (*See p. 33, ante.*)

has already been at least six days since the whole category
of conditions for moving forward and taking Richmond has
been fulfilled, and six days since an additional condition
turned up in his favor—the reinforcing of Jackson at Gordonsville, *from Richmond*—it has been two days since he
learned that the powerful corps of Jackson, thus reinforced,
was but two or three days march off, on his way to join Lee,)
" the enemy attacked our right in force, and turned my attention to the protection of our *communications and depots
of supply ;*" both of which, by the by, were lost, and were
*expected to be lost*, since he telegraphs the Secretary of War
" not to be discouraged if you learn that my communications
are cut off *and even Yorktown in possession of the enemy.*"

Now, on the morning of the 26th, Jackson's main body
was yet a *full day's march* off.  It was noon on the 26th,
(p. 124,) before the enemy was discovered to be in motion,
and 3 P. M., (p. 125,) before he had "formed his line of battle" to attack McCall, at Beaver Dam Creek.  The troops
which attacked on the 26th were not Jackson's, but *a part
of the very force Gen. McClellan was to have attacked himself.*  Thus we learn the curious and astonishing fact that
the "general forward movement," or, as styled, p. 122, "our
final advance decided upon for that day," was postponed and
abandoned *in consequence of an attack of the enemy's which
took place at 3 P. M. of the same day !*

Now if the case was really hopeless, we would fold our
hands in resignation, only asking why the conclusion was not
arrived at three weeks earlier ; for we affirm that nothing
happened up to the 26th to make a " moving forward and
taking Richmond" more impracticable than when Gen. Mc-
Clellan, (on the 7th,) announced that he should be "in perfect readiness" when McCall arrived and the ground dried—
conditions all fulfilled as early as the 20th. (12)  Even to the
25th nothing that has occurred has daunted the ostensible
determination to "advance and take Richmond," and a
grand "preparatory" movement to a "general forward
movement" was ordered.  But man cannot control events,
and who could forbode that, almost simultaneously with the

order for " an advance of our picket line of the left preparatory, &c., &c.," *several contrabands* would be on their way
with tidings of Beauregard and Jackson! that a " final advance " for to-morrow, (the 26th,) will be utterly frustrated
by a *counter* advance made by a disobliging enemy *at 3
o'clock in the afternoon of that day !*

Truly " the case is a difficult one," but we need not lose
hope, for the General will do his best to " out-manœuver,
out-wit and out-fight the enemy."

With an army of 100,000 men *present for duty*—an enemy
divided into two portions, even if " greatly superior in number," we would fancy *something* might be done, even had we
not this voluntary pledge of brilliant generalship. Indeed it
has been our notion that these were just the circumstances
that called for energetic action—a prompt and bold *initiative*
on the part of a general.

Admitting that the enemy really numbered, (as is stated
on the authority of the "secret service,") 180,000 men, and
admitting that the " advance " on Richmond had ceased to
be practicable, and that a retreat to the James River had
become the best course, why amuse us in this official *Report*
of *past* events with the pretence, kept up till the 25th, nay,
to the 26th, of a "general forward movement?" Such a
movement was surely more practicable while Jackson was at
Gordonsville, or even when only three marches off, than
when he arrived. Why, *if really intended*, was it not made ?

In view of a retreat to the James River it was wise to hold
the position at Beaver Dam on the 26th. All Porter's baggage
train might have been, (and we believe *was*,) brought over
on that day. So might have been the " siege guns." It was
a blunder unparalleled to expose Porter's corps to fight a
battle by itself on the 27th against overwhelming forces of
the enemy. With perfect ease that corps might have been
brought over on the night of the 26th, and, if nothing more
brilliant could have been thought of, the movement to the
James might have been in full tide of execution on the 27th.
A more propitious moment could not have been chosen, for,
besides Jackson's own forces, A. P. Hill's and Longstreet's

corps were on the south (left) bank of the Chickahominy on the night of the 26th. Such a movement need not have been discovered to the enemy till far enough advanced to insure success. At any rate he could have done no better in preventing it than he actually did afterwards. The Prince de Joinville, conceding the necessity of the movement says, "there was a vast difference between making this *retreat*," (styling it very properly what it was,) "in one's own time and by a free, spontaneous movement, and making it hastily under the threatening pressure of two hostile armies;" and surely the difference became vaster when, instead of being made merely *under pressure*, it became the necessary result of a decided defeat.

But the enemy had no such numbers, nor was the case so hopeless. The "secret service," which reported the incredible number of 100,000 men under Johnston, at Manassas, is authority for the 180,000 now massed against Gen. McClellan; but it also reports the force made up of two hundred battalions of infantry and cavalry and eight battalions of "independent troops," five battalions of artillery and some fragmentary bodies. Now, 500 men to a battalion was a *full estimate*, and so recognized by the "secret service." Out of the organizations enumerated it would, therefore, be hard to make a total of more than 110,000 or 115,000 men, while our own aggregate (sick and well) is given by Gen. McClellan (p. 11) at 117,000. Wm. Henry Hurlbert, who had been in Richmond throughout the campaign, and had had excellent opportunities of judging, gives his opinion that Lee's army numbered 90,000, and Jackson's, 30,000, making 120,000 in all. Mr. Hurlbert also says: "Very few, if any, of his (Beauregard's) troops were in Virginia." In other words, he knew of none at all, and there has never been furnished a particle of proof that a single man of Beauregard's army was there.

But even Mr. Hurlbert's estimate is largely in excess. The divisions of Longstreet, A. P. Hill and D. H. Hill, and the corps of Jackson, were, as we know, engaged in the action with Porter on the 27th, and this force has been estimated from 60,000 to 70,000 men. The Richmond papers of that date, describing the battle, stated it at 65,000 men, and the probability is that it did not vary much from that. The enemy made his effort upon our right under Porter, and naturally concentrated against it all the troops he could spare, while keeping up a show of force about Richmond. Independently of such an inference, we have the fact that Gen. Magruder, in his official report, describes the situation of the rebel forces left on the Richmond side as "one of the gravest peril," and states that "there were but 25,000 men between McClellan's army of 100,000 men and Richmond." (13) The same Richmond paper which, a few days after the battles, mentioned the amount of Confederate force (as above stated) engaged with Porter, speculated upon *what might have happened* had McClellan on the 27th *attacked Richmond.* The rebel Gen. Stuart, in an interview with a distinguished officer of our army which occurred a few weeks after these events, *pledged his honor* that the Confederate force did not exceed 90,000 men. That he *knew* what that force was is certain, and it is not likely that he would tell a gratuitous falsehood. Nothing that occurred in any of the encounters during the seven days, or afterwards, warrants the belief that the Confederate army exceeded that number. The *very same* corps and divisions which, on the left of the Chickahominy, fought Porter at Gaines' Mill, turn up, with Magruder and Huger alone added, at the fierce and momentous combats of Glendale and Malvern Hill.

Conceding, however, to Gen. McClellan an adversary which his "secret service," aided by "several contrabands," had conjured up, the passive inactivity with which he met this crisis forfeits for him every claim to generalship even of the most indifferent character. With an enemy 180,000 strong, divided into two distinct portions, we believe that there might have been found some way of displaying generalship; at least, with intrenchments on the right bank of the Chickahominy which 20,000 men could have held against 100,000, he need not have permitted one-third of his army to be defeated on the other bank, within sight and cannon range of the other two-thirds. But, considering the *real strength* of his enemy, (as we believe it to have been,) a more lamentable failure to fulfill " hopes formerly placed in him," a more striking instance, not so much of being " outwitted" as of destitution of " wit," and of unreadiness in action, is scarcely to be found in military annals.

The enemy having been checked at Beaver Dam Creek in the afternoon of the 26th, no time should have been lost in withdrawing from this position and in bringing Porter over the Chickahominy, as could have been done with the greatest ease the night of the 26th. If it had been determined, however, to fight on that side, he should have been withdrawn in the night to the position selected, and at the same time reinforced with the whole of our right wing, except 20,000 men to hold the intrenchments and Bottom's Bridge, and to guard the passages of the White Oak Swamp. Thirty or forty thousand men should have been sent over to Porter. (14)

Gen. McCall, who commanded the force at Beaver Dam Creek which received the rebel attack under A. P. Hill on the 26th, says, in reference to the order to withdraw : " This order, I confess, gave me some concern. *Had it reached me at midnight*, the movement might have been made without difficulty and without loss; but now it would be daylight before the movement which, under fire, is one of the most delicate and difficult in the art of war, could be commenced."

The movement, ordered at nightfall of the 26th, could have been executed without risk or damage. Delayed till morning, it involved the risk of the utter destruction of Porter's corps of 27,000 men. Not a *slight* risk merely, such as we must constantly incur in making war, but a serious risk, and, moreover, a totally unnecessary one. Porter acknowledged his hesitation to give the order for withdrawing his force, and even seemed, when morning came, inclined to suspend it, alleging the fear that McCall's division would be *cut to pieces*. Not only McCall's division, but Porter's whole command, were in fearful risk of being " cut to pieces" or captured, by being where they were that morning of the 27th, as we shall show.

Gen. Stoneman, with a small command of infantry and cavalry, had been sent towards " Old Church" to obstruct roads, destroy bridges, and prevent, as far as possible, Porter's right from being turned. Jackson, who, in marching from Hanover C. H., kept well towards the Pamunkey, with the obvious intention of turning Porter's right, on coming in sight of Stoneman's troops near " Old Church," bore off towards Mechanicsville. His troops filed past in full view of Stoneman from 4 P. M. till after dark, and were estimated by him at 35,000 strong. (Jackson *now* had, besides his own troops, those "reinforcements" which we have seen were sent a week or two ago, out of Richmond, to join him.) Let us suppose that Jackson, instead of being diverted from his course by the handful of troops of Stoneman, (and it is astonishing that he should have been,) had kept on towards Cold Harbor. Porter's case would have been hopeless.

He bore off towards Mechanicsville, and encamped somewhere near Shady Grove Church. Had he put his troops in motion before dawn and marched parallel to Porter's line of retreat, he could have attacked his retiring columns and rendered it difficult, if not impossible, for him to reach the position where he actually gave battle. Finally, that the force of Porter was not utterly destroyed by its defeat, is due simply to the fact (not to have been expected) that the enemy did not commence his attack till 3½ P. M., and did not accomplish his victory until after nightfall. These, it may be urged, were *risks* incidental to war; but they were risks of the gravest character, and we are unable to see what equivalent risks (rather than positive advantages) would have attended the withdrawal of Porter the night of the 26th.

Gen. McClellan announces that " the object we sought for had been obtained." " The enemy was held at bay." (But why incur a disastrous defeat to hold him "at bay" in a position where he could not attack us unless we chose to be attacked.) " Our siege guns and materials *were saved.*" (Everything was brought over on the 26th except the siege guns, and they might have been,) "and the right wing now joined the main body of the army," (which it might have done the night of the 26th.")

*Per contra*, we lost twenty-two guns "captured by the enemy," (better have abandoned and spiked the "siege artillery" than to have lost *in battle* twenty two guns.) We lost in killed and wounded 9,000 men, when Porter might have been withdrawn without the loss of a man, and we incurred a disheartening defeat besides. (15)

As to the answers of the corps commanders to the circular of the 26th, asking if they could spare troops to reinforce Porter, we need hardly remark that when circulars of this kind are sent to commanding officers, one style of answer only can be anticipated. Each commander, without precise knowledge of the situation, or of the plans of the general, feels bound to provide for the worst possible case. No one has any troops to spare. It is for the *commanding general himself* to decide, in view of his own plans, how many men are wanted at different points, and with how many each shall be held. Now it may be safely said that the "defensive works" on the right bank of the Chickahominy could be held with 20,000 men against 100,000. They were built, (as explained by Gen. McClellan himself,) "that he might bring the greatest possible numbers into action," and, built in this view, they must have had some considerable strength. Gen. Barnard describes these lines as consisting of six redoubts, connected by rifle pits or barricades. These rifle pits were in fact infantry parapets, raised to the height of the breast above the natural surface, the ditch or excavation being on the outside. The redoubts were arranged with embrasures and had in several cases *magazines* provided. The woods outside the lines were felled and formed, along the greater portion, an obstacle impossible to be passed under fire of the works. Gen. McClellan, in his brief report of July 15th, (which he has not inserted in this volume) saw fit to style these defences "slight earthworks,"—a term which one would apply to such works as troops could throw up in a night. On these our troops had been working for twenty five days, and he himself has stated the object of their construction, (p. 118,) and by his manner of speaking of them has indicated that they were not a night's work, but a serious labor. (16) *Why* he afterwards styles them, disparagingly, "slight earthworks" is very apparent. It would be otherwise unintelligible why 70,000 effective men lay idle behind them, while, within cannon shot, 27,000 were undergoing a disastrous defeat.

Two defensive battles have now been fought on the Chickahominy, and Gen. McClellan has either blundered into fighting them, or been *compelled*, by the circumstances of his position, to fight them, the first with about one-half, the second with less than one-third, of his force; and now, (not a single offensive action having occurred during this invasive campaign,) with a "splendid army," as he rightly styles it, he is forced, though still superior, or at least equal in numbers, to "change his base," or, in other words, to beat a retreat.

He has spent weeks in building bridges which establish a close connection between the wings of his army, and then fights a great battle with a smaller fraction of his army than when he had a single available bridge, and that remote. He, with great labor, constructs "defensive works" in order that he "may bring the greatest possible numbers into action," and again exhibits his ability to utilize his means by keeping 65,000 men idle behind them, while 35,000, unaided by "defensive works" of any kind, fight the bulk of his adversary's forces, and are of course overwhelmed by "superior numbers."

We believe there were few commanding officers of the Army of the Potomac who did not expect to be led *offensively* against the enemy on the 26th or 27th. (17) Had such a movement been made it is not improbable that, if energetically led, we should have gone into Richmond. Jackson and A. P. Hill could not have got back in time to succor Magruder's command, if measures of most obvious propriety had been taken to prevent them. We might have beaten or driven Magruder's 25,000 men and entered Richmond, and then reinforced by the great *moral* acquisition of strength this success would have given, have fought Lee and re-established our communications. At any rate *something* of this kind was worth trying. (18)

The story of the campaign is nearly told. What follows is but the denouement. The retreat to the James River, considering that the bulk of the enemy was on the left bank of the Chickahominy, and that he had a long march before he could reach our flank, was not very difficult. The troops were moved judiciously, and were put in position at the most obvious points; but so far as the "fighting" is concerned it is as usual, pellmell, no one knowing exactly who and where his neighbor is, and what is worse, *no common head near at hand*, who does know all, to direct and give coherence and unity to the operations.

On the 30th of June our army stretched across the country from White Oak Swamp bridge to the James, occupying a line about eight miles long. Franklin held the right at the bridge, Porter and Keyes the extreme left. Farther than midway (five miles about) from the James, this long line of battle was intersected by two, (the "Charles City" and the "New Market" or "Long Bridge") converging roads. Here was *the decisive point*—if the line should be broken here it would be the destruction of our army. Here, too, the enemy made a desperate effort. Lee commanded in person, and Longstreet's and A. P. Hill's veteran divisions, numbering 18 to 20,000 men, made the attack. Jeff Davis himself was said to be present. (So Gen. McCall, while a prisoner that evening, was informed). It was an eventful day and an eventful point; central, too, to the general position of the army. Where was the Commanding General during this battle? At the very extreme left, and for a considerable portion of the time *on a gunboat*, (see p. 135,) "having made arrangements for instant communication by signals." Read the report of Gen. McCall, the extracts from those of Sumner, and Heintzelman, and others, and their testimony before the Committee on the Conduct of the War, and see how much the control of the Commanding General was needed;

his knowledge of the field and of the positions of the different troops. Then think of the disastrous consequences that would have followed the breaking of our line at that point, (Longstreet informed Gen. McCall that Lee had 70,000 men bearing on it, all of which would arrive before midnight,) and let each one form his own conclusion as to whether the commanding General had on this occasion any appreciation of his duties, or, if he had, whether he discharged them.

"It was very late at night," says Gen. McClellan, "before my aids returned to give me *the results of the day's fighting along the whole line, and the true position of affairs.*" It may well be doubted whether, in all the recorded reports or "dispatches" of military commanders, a parallel to this extraordinary avowal can be found. We supposed it the especial business of a general to know, at each moment, "the true position of affairs," and to have some agency in ruling it. Here we find the "day's fighting" all done, the results, for better or worse, accomplished, and "very late at night" the commanding General just learning about them! "Very late at night" Gen. Franklin *concluded* he could no longer hold his position and retired, sending word to Gens. Sumner and Heintzelman. These officers, though they assert they received no such message, heard of the movement, somehow, and wisely concluded that they must retire, too. Here again was a matter of the gravest importance, which, that it should be decided at the proper time, required the commanding General to be at hand—to know, promptly, "the situation" and the "results of the day's fighting." Gen. McClellan makes no pretence that he gave any orders to Franklin, nor that he would have given any to the other corps commanders had not Franklin, *without orders*, fallen back. He affirms that on learning of Franklin's withdrawal he *sent orders* to Sumner and Heintzelman to withdraw, but admits that they were both in motion *without his orders*. (19) Now had *not* this withdrawal taken place that night, the next day would have probably witnessed the destruction of the Army of the Potomac. Lee, as we have seen, was at the very central point, ready to break in, with a force of 70,000 men, as stated by Longstreet to Gen. McCall. The salvation of the army was due, not to McClellan's arrangements or foresight, but to Gen. Franklin's fortunate decision to withdraw. The army was saved *in spite* of Gen. McClellan's ignorance of the "position of affairs" and "results of the day's fighting," and consequent incapacity to give intelligent orders. (20)

Our army is now concentrated on the James; but we have another day's fighting before us, and this day we may expect the concentrated attack of Lee's whole army. We know not at what hour it will come—possibly late, for it requires time to find out our new position and to bring together the attacking columns—yet we know not when it will come. Where, *this* day, is the commanding General? Off, with Capt. Rodgers, to select "the final positions of the army and its depots." He does not tell us that it was on a gunboat, and that this day not even "signals" would keep him in communication with his army, for his journey was ten or fifteen miles down the river; and he was thus absent till late in the afternoon. (21)

This is the first time we ever had reason to believe that the highest and first duty of a general, on the day of battle, was, separating himself from his army, to reconnoitre a place of retreat! However that may be, that night and the day following, the whole army, with the exception of Gen. Keyes' corps, marched into a cul-de-sac from which it could not have been extricated had the enemy been able promptly to follow us up.

We think it will now be understood why "a large number of Gen. McClellan's highest officers—indeed a majority of those whose opinions have been reported to me," (see Gen. Halleck's letter, p. 157) are in favor of "the withdrawal from the James." If the enemy *was* indeed, as Gen. McClellan estimated, (Gen. Halleck's letter, p. 156) 200,000 strong, and daily increasing, a renewal of an offensive campaign from the James was simple madness. *Once*, by his own accounts, he had been foiled and driven back, with no little hazard of the ruin of his army, by "superior numbers," and now he proposes to march again with 120,000 (about what his army would have numbered with the 30,000 reinforcements he asked) against Richmond, held by 200,000 men. No one who has read attentively the report before us, and the dispatches therein contained, will be surprised at the want of logical sequence in any particular plan, statement or argument, since complete destitution of such a quality is the characteristic of the whole; but any intelligent reader will understand that there were no rational chances of success, particularly after recent experiences, in " advancing on Richmond" defended by an army of 200,000 men inured to battles and elated by success, with but 120,000 men. (22) He can understand, too, that *another* disastrous repulse in this region was likely to result in the loss of the army and the capture of Washington—indeed, the ruin of the cause.

If the enemy had 200,000 men it was to be seriously apprehended that, leaving 50,000 behind the "strong works" of Richmond, he would march at once with 150,000 men on Washington. Why should he not? Gen. McClellan and his eulogists have held up as highly meritorious strategy the leaving of Washington defended by less than 50,000 men, with the enemy in its front estimated to be 120,000 to 150,000 strong, and moving off to take an eccentric line of operations against Richmond; and now the *reverse case is presented*, but with an important difference. The enemy at Manassas, on learning Gen. McClellan's movement, could either fly to the defence of Richmond or attack Washington. *Gen. McClellan says that this latter course was not to be feared.* McClellan on the James, on learning that Lee with 150,000 men is marching on Washington, *can only* attack Richmond; by no possibility can he fly to the defence of Washington. Besides, he is inferior in numbers (according to his own estimate) even to Lee's marching army. Here, in a nutshell, is the demonstration of the folly of the grand strategic movement on Richmond, as given by its own projector.

If the enemy had nothing like 200,000 men—(and a very

reliable estimate put his forces in the early part of August at about 55,000 *around Richmond*, and the rest with Jackson confronting Pope, probably not more than 40,000)—if he never had had more than 90,000, or at the utmost 120,000—if Gen. McClellan had been driven away from Richmond by equal or inferior numbers, there were still strong reasons, (which we need not indicate,) after the recent experience undergone, for not permitting him to incur the hazard of another advance.

The critical situation of affairs at this period, the urgent necessity of providing for the safety of Washington and of effecting the reunion into one whole of our shattered and reduced armies in Virginia, demanded imperatively the withdrawal from the James. The great misfortune was that the order was not given immediately on our reaching Harrison's Landing.

Had Gen. McClellan made his " reports " of the various actions of the Army of the Potomac as they occurred, he would probably have done himself more credit, (though the slight specimen we have in his report made July 15th, of the seven days' battles hardly warrants this opinion,) than he has by this laborious but disingenuous production. He has, however, done the country and done history a service. In giving so many of his own dispatches he has furnished the truest tests of his actual abilities as a general and a thinker, and in the matter and in the arrangement of it he has given us an illustration of his animus as a historian. In this point of view the Report may be safely recommended to readers of all classes and all parties. In taking leave of the Army of the Potomac he somewhat ostentatiously promised to make himself the historian of its exploits, and we have before us now, in the pages we have just examined, the result of his six months' incubation on such a theme.

" Whoever has committed no faults has not made war " was the remark of one of the great marshals of France when questioned as to the cause of a defeat, and acknowledging it to have been the result of his own mistakes ; and there would have been no lack of indulgence and charity for the failure of an inexperienced subaltern suddenly converted into a general, and called upon to plan campaigns and direct armies of such unusual magnitude, under circumstances of no ordinary difficulty, were they presented to us in the spirit of Marshal Turenne's avowal; but when exactly the reverse is the case, when the claim to eminent generalship is arrogantly asserted, when plans which we have shown to be lacking in the essential elements of consistency in themselves, and of concert with those who must be depended upon to carry them out, are held up for our admiration, when all faults are denied and the burden of each particular mishap, and, in the end, of the failure of the whole campaign, is thrown upon the administration; when, in short, the whole Report is one incessant complaint against the President and the War Department, culminating at length in the outrageous charge addressed to the Secretary of War on the eve of Porter's defeat, (a fit *finale* to the two days' blundering,) "You have done your best to sacrifice this army," we think charity should withdraw her mantle from the errors and inconsistencies and incapacity which we here exhibit.

# APPENDIX.

THE interest attached to the origin, motives, and causes of that plan of campaign which removed the Army of the Potomac from its primitive base to the lower Chesapeake, induces me to add the following " Memoranda" furnished to Gen. McClellan.

On one of the last days of November, 1861, I was at Gen. McClellan's Head-quarters, and found myself alone with him. Casually, apparently, he mentioned the plan he had recently conceived of moving the army, by water, to the Rappahannock. The features of the plan, as I now recollect, were, principally, these: to carry the whole, or at least the greater part, of the army, to Urbanna, by water, and by a rapid march to cut off and " bag" Magruder's force on the peninsula—seize Richmond, all before Johnston's force from Manassas could arrive to succor it. To prevent, or at least delay the arrival of that army, the " railroad bridges" of the different roads between Richmond and Manassas were, at the proper moment, to be destroyed. The General intimated that he had agents to do this work upon whom he could rely. (23)

The " memoranda" following, of the 5th and 6th of December, are the results of my reflections on that plan.

About the middle of January 1862 I was directed to see Col. Ingalls in reference to water " transportation" for troops. The memorandum of January 13th was written after consultation with that officer. The tenor of the paper will show that I had no positive knowledge of the *object* for which such transportation was to be collected; but suspecting that object, I took occasion to repeat my strong convictions of the injudiciousness of such a step.

When, early in March, 1862, I formed one of a council of war of twelve general officers to whom, by order of the President, this important question was submitted, I had no other intimation of a serious intention to make such a movement than the casual mention of it to me by Gen. McClellan, in the latter part of November. Not having any reason to suppose that any officer of the council had any more intimate knowledge of the intention than myself, and knowing how much thought the slight intimation I had received had cost me, I naturally expected deliberation and discussion. To my great surprise, eight of the twelve officers present voted, off hand, *for* the measure, *without* discussion; nor was any argument on my part available to obtain a reconsideration.

*Memorandum for General McClellan (written and sent 5th of December, 1861).*

The idea of shifting the theatre of operations to the James, York, or Rappahannock has often occurred. The great difficulty I have found in this matter is that of moving a body as large as necessary rapidly, and of making the necessary preparations for such a movement so that they should not, in themselves, give indications of the whereabouts of the intended operations in time to meet them.

The first thing to be considered is the *old* danger attending all similar operations. In cutting the enemy's line of operations you expose yourself—and a bold and desperate enemy, seeing himself anticipated at Richmond, might attempt to retrieve the disaster by a desperate effort upon Washington. Leaving, then, as we should do, the great mass of the enemy in front of Washington, it would not be safe to leave it guarded by less than 100,000 men—that is, until we became certain that he had withdrawn from our front, so far as to render his return upon it impracticable. It seems to me too, that the *full garrisoning* of the works up to the standard fixed upon should be completed without delay. These works will but imperfectly serve their purpose if they are not defended by troops who have some familiarity with their positions.

   *      *      *      *      *      *      *      *

I dwell on this matter somewhat, since if the army moves—*particularly* if it makes a flank movement leaving the enemy in front—the measures for defence of the city can not be too carefully taken.

Now as to the expedition. Considering the great difficulty of transporting, *at one time*, large numbers—the confusion which will attend the landing, and consequent difficulty of getting the columns into prompt *marching* order after landing, with our new troops, if the numbers are great—I should be disposed to make the first descent with a comparatively small but select corps—not over 20, at outside 30,000 men.

Let it be supposed the latter number is adopted—how shall the movement be made so as to attract least attention in its preparations and to deceive the enemy as to their object ?

Gen. Burnside's force I *suppose* to be about 10,000 men. His flotilla, including his seven sailing vessels and five " floating batteries," will carry that number. (In my former memorandum I estimated 14,350, but I now exclude the " surf boats" and " launches," and diminish the numbers, as I then estimated for a short voyage *not leaving* the Potomac.)

I suppose there would be three batteries and say 1,000 cavalry accompanying this division. I suppose that among the large steamers about Baltimore the additional transportation for this artillery and cavalry could be found. If so, we have a force of 10,000 or 11,000, with artillery and cavalry, provided for.

For a second column, I think I would embark it from the Port Tobacco River. The concentration of troops under Hooker would cover a movement that way, and it would threaten the Potomac batteries.

Now for additional numbers. I am inclined to think it is easier to carry troops to New York (12 hours)—embark them there, and make but one thing of it—than to bring the shipping to Annapolis or the Potomac.

However that may be, if it is determined that the additional number shall be 10,000 men or 20,000 men, or more, I would command the transportation at once in New York—the place where *every thing* can be had in unstinted quantities and of the most suitable kind. All sea steamers (not otherwise chartered), the large Sound steamers, the large North River, Sound and coasting propellers, can be had there, and there all the appliances to fit them for troops, horses, etc., can be quickest made.

Perhaps the best way, therefore, would be to commence at once and send the troops, artillery, and cavalry, to Fort Monroe—to hold themselves ready for shipment at a moment's notice—to order the transportation necessary in New York.

According to the foregoing propositions, there would be three columns ready for a simultaneous movement—10,000 at Annapolis, 10,000 at Port Tobacco River, and 10 or 20,000 at Fort Monroe. The times of starting could be arranged so that the times of arrival should be as desired. Probably it would be better to have more than one point of debarkation.

As soon as the first columns were landed, the transports could go immediately to Annapolis or Baltimore for more.

The arrangements give no indication of the intended point of attack. They threaten the Potomac, or Norfolk, or the Southern coast, as much as, or more than, the Rappahannock.

I presume there would be no difficulty in sending our steamers down to Port Tobacco—whether there would be in towing the barges there I do not know. This Potomac column does not satisfy me as well as the others, for the collection of troops at Port Tobacco, *in connection* with collections at Fort Monroe and Annapolis, would rather indicate an operation in the lower Chesapeake.

Distances of points mentioned to Urbanna. Annapolis 120 miles—Port Tobacco 90—Fort Monroe 60.

Respectfully submitted,

J. G. B.

*Memorandum.*

WASHINGTON, December 6, 1861.

MY DEAR GENERAL :—

When you suggested to me a Southern movement I told you that my ideas had turned towards Norfolk.

Its capture would not be so great an operation as the *successful* execution of the project you propose—still it seems to me worthy of consideration as attended with less risk. To execute successfully the operation you propose with a moderate army (say 20 or 30,000 men) to be afterwards reinforced, depends upon auxiliary aids which *may* fail.

If the railroad bridges are not destroyed—or but imperfectly— the enemy may overwhelm our expeditionary army—while to execute the difficult operation of transferring at once a *large* army—say 100,000 men to that line, I look upon as impracticable, if not otherwise imprudent.

There is one very important consideration in this matter of changing the line of operations. The army of the Potomac has an object of immense importance to defend—the *Capital*, to lose which would be almost to lose everything.

We *cannot* withdraw the bulk of the army from Washington with the enemy in our front—I would not trust enough to its fortifications for *that.*

On the other hand the enemy in front has nothing to defend. If we throw 30 or 50,000 men on to the Rappahannock, he can abandon entirely his position at Manassas, and have object enough to do so in the hope of overwhelming our force—and I think it is too great a hazard to risk, upon the expectation of his railroad bridges being destroyed.

There is another operation which I should think well worthy of weighing. To throw an army of 30,000 men on to Norfolk, landing between the Elizabeth and Nansemond. The enemy's army at Norfolk would be cut off. The Nansemond and Dismal Swamp would, I should judge by the map, give us a defensive line against the enemy's reinforcements, (breaking the railroad as far as possible) and the capture of Norfolk would be, if not so brilliant and decisive as what you propose, yet a great blow, particularly if, at the same time, we captured its army. At the same time a demonstration in force on the enemy in our front would either prevent his making detachments, or compel him to abandon his position and his batteries on the Potomac.

Respectfully submitted,<br>J. G. Barnard.

### Memorandum for General McClellan.

WASHINGTON, January 13th, 1862.

On consultation with Col. Ingalls, who says he has been engaged in investigating this subject for several weeks, and has visited the Northern cities, he tells me that for an expedition to be made in *smooth water* (such as the Potomac or even the Chesapeake) transportation can be collected at Annapolis for *one* division of 12 regiments infantry—1 regiment (1000) cavalry with horses—4 batteries artillery horses and men—one ponton bridge train, say 70 six-horse wagons, horses, drivers and 2 companies pontoniers—and 250 quarter-master wagons, ambulances, with provisions for one week—*in three weeks' time.*

He thinks that more than one division could not be simultaneously embarked without withdrawing vessels in service of the Government elsewhere.

In this estimate, however, Col. Ingalls does not include some 10 or 15 clipper ships which could be had and which draw too much water to approach the shore, or to enter shallow bays or rivers. I should not think this objection decisive, since there is water enough in the Chesapeake, Potomac, Rappahannock or York, for such vessels, and they need not approach the shores ; the landing of troops can be effected through the aid of the lighter vessels of the other division.

If these ships are employed, as well as lighter vessels, another division—two in all can be simultaneously embarked—and it would require four (4) weeks to have them all at Annapolis ready to receive troops.

In this estimate, I understand, are included Sound steamers North River steamers, propellers, canal barges and tow boats (from New York and Philadelphia), and, in fact, everything that would be available in a limited time, fit for the purpose.

As Col. Ingalls has made this subject his study, I presume I am justified in saying that transportation for two, and only two, divisions can be assembled at Annapolis in four weeks. If craft of light draught alone are demanded, transportation for only one can be had, and that can be furnished in three weeks.

With reference to what can be found here, I have stated in my memorandum of December that the Navy had (or did have not long ago) four side-wheel steamers and the steamer " Stepping Stones" capable of carrying 3,500 men, and the quarter-master's department had two large steamers and some smaller ones capable of carrying (as stated to me by Col. Rucker) 5,000 men, besides several large Schuylkill barges. I learn that there are, on the Chesapeake and Ohio Canal, between here and Cumberland, from 250 to 300 good canal boats, 90 feet long, $14\frac{1}{2}$ beam, and about 6 feet depth ; they will carry 150 to 200 men each.

During the present mild weather these boats could be got down the canal, and they would carry troops, but they are ill adapted to carrying horses. Besides these canal boats and vessels in employ of the Government, there is very little else to be found here now.

But it is impracticable to move large bodies of men, on vessels of this kind, past the enemy's batteries on the Potomac, and hence, troops could be moved from here only to points *above* such batteries.

If Col. Ingalls' statement is taken as a basis of our resources in this matter, it ensues that without withdrawing vessels from other service of the Government, the means cannot be obtained, that is, speedily, to transport four or five divisions *at one time.*

It seems likely that two divisions could be simultaneously transported, and the same means be used to bring on very speedily thereafter two more divisions, &c.

The proposition to move four or five divisions by water, seems to imply the transfer of the base of active operations from here to some other point, as the Rappahannock or York Rivers.

On this point I would refer to memoranda of December 5th and 6th. This investigation of the matter of water transportation has confirmed my previous impressions of the difficulty of making such a transfer without unmistakable indications which would enable the enemy, in great measure, to prepare for it. The cost of such a transfer cannot be less than one or two millions.*

We have now our base established here. In operating upon the enemy's centre at Occoquan we cannot fail to break it, or force him to abandon Northern Virginia, or give us battle. On this line we have the Potomac by which to do most of our heavy transportation, thus palliating the winter difficulty of bad roads. We have the Potomac flotilla to aid our operations. (If a few of the new regular gunboats could be added, it would be a great advantage.)

Forcing the line of the Occoquan we shall at once clear the Potomac of the enemy's batteries, and from Aquia and Fredericksburg, have a convenient base of operations against Richmond.

Simultaneously with the passage of the Occoquan, Sickles' brigade might cross to Mathias Point; that position is, I should judge, very defensible, and from it, if circumstances favored, the batteries at Potomac and Aquia Creek could be captured.

J. G. B.

---

* The *actual* cost of the transfer of the army to the Peninsula was many times this conjectural amount.

# NOTES.

## Note 1.—Page 4.

The following paragraphs from the well-known letter of Lord Lyons, to his government, dated Washington, November 17, 1862, very clearly illustrate the identification of Gen. McClellan with the party to which I allude; and they illustrate too, the views and objects of " leaders " of that party.

That Gen. McClellan's dismissal " dashed their hopes" in more senses than one is very true—for, from the very beginning, it was through his influence over the army that it was intended and hoped that that powerful political element should be wielded against the administration. Whether or not the administration had thrown itself into the hands of the " extreme Radical party," it is very evident that it had ample cause to desire no longer the services of Gen. McClellan (as will clearly appear in the text of this review), especially as that officer himself had " thrown himself into the hands" of its political opponents.

" On the following morning, however, intelligence arrived from Washington which dashed the rising hopes of the conservatives. It was announced that Gen. McClellan had been dismissed from the command of the Army of the Potomac, and ordered to repair to his home ; that he had, in fact, been removed altogether from active service. The General had been regarded as the representative of conservative principle in the army. Support of him had been made one of the articles of the conservative electoral programme. His dismissal was taken as a sign that the President had thrown himself entirely into the arms of the extreme Radical party, and that the attempt to carry out the policy of that party would be persisted in. The irritation of the Conservatives at New York was certainly very great; it seemed, however, to be not unmixed with consternation and despondency.

" Several of the leaders of the Democratic party sought interviews with me, both before and after the arrival of the intelligence of Gen. McClellan's dismissal. The subject uppermost in their minds while they were speaking to me was naturally that of foreign mediation between the North and South. Many of them seemed to think that this mediation must come at last; but they appeared to be very much afraid of its coming too soon. It was evident that they apprehended that a premature proposal of foreign intervention would afford the Radical party a means of reviving the violent war spirit, and of thus defeating the peaceful plans of the Conservatives. They appeared to regard the present movement as peculiarly unfavorable for such an offer, and, indeed, to hold that it would be essential to the success of any proposal from abroad that it should be deferred until the control of the Executive Government should be in the hands of the Conservative party.

"I gave no opinion on the subject. I did not say whether or not I myself thought foreign intervention probable or advisable; but I listened with attention to the accounts given me of the plans and hopes of the Conservative party. *At the bottom I thought I perceived a desire to put an end to the war, even at the risk of losing the Southern States altogether;* but it was plain that it was not thought prudent to avow this desire. Indeed, some hints of it, dropped before the elections, were so ill received that a strong declaration in the contrary sense was deemed necessary by the Democratic leaders.

"At the present moment, therefore, the chiefs of the Conservative party call loudly for a more vigorous prosecution of the war, and reproach the Government with slackness as well as with want of success in its military measures."

---

## NOTE 2.—PAGE 12.

In his evidence before the Committee on the Conduct of the War we find the following:

"*Question.* Would not the destruction of the Merrimac have been a great point gained, and have rendered the movement upon Richmond, by way of the James or York Rivers, very much more safe?"

"*Answer.* As things turned out, yes. But I do not think that the importance of the Merrimac was appreciated until she came out. I remember very well that the Navy Department thought that the Congress and Cumberland were capable of taking care of the Merrimac."

That two *sailing* vessels lying at anchor should be capable of "taking care" of a powerful iron-clad steamer is an idea which ought not to be attributed to the Navy Department. That Department knew of the conversion of the Merrimac into an iron-clad, and had painful forebodings of the consequences, and it was at the suggestion of the Assistant Secretary, Mr. Fox, that I drew up, for him, in February, the memorandum on the " taking of Norfolk," alluded to in the following letter :

*Letter of Mr. Fox.*

"WASHINGTON, April 30, 1864.

" DEAR SIR—I have the honor of enclosing herewith copies of a letter from the senior officer at Hampton Roads, called for with reference to the anxiety of this Department constantly manifested to attack Norfolk and thereby get rid of the Merrimac. Also a letter of Rear-Admiral Goldsborough, which will acquaint you with the Navy impression as to the Merrimac.

" The frigate Congress, having half a crew, was ordered to leave Newport News, but at the earnest request of Gen. Wool, who put men on board from the marine brigade, she was detained, but the steam-tugs to attend the Congress and Cumberland in case of an attack were not on hand when she came out.

" My impression of your memorandum about the taking of Norfolk is, that it was made at my request, that our design of taking Norfolk should receive the weight of your judgment when presented to Gen. McClellan. The General admitted its force, but took no action.  Yours, very truly,

(*Signed*)  G. V. Fox.

BRIGADIER-GENERAL JOHN G. BARNARD, U. S. Army.

Washington, D. C.

*Extract from a Letter of Admiral Goldsborough.*

" (*Confidential.*)  U. S. FLAG-SHIP MINNESOTA,
HAMPTON ROADS, October 17, 1861.

SIR—I have received further minute reliable information with regard to the preparation of the Merrimac for an attack on Newport

News and these roads, as I am now quite satisfied that unless her stability be compromitted by her heavy top works of wood and iron, and her weight of battery, she will, in all probability, prove to be very formidable. The supposition of the insurgents is that she will be impregnable, and a trial of her sufficiency to resist shot of the heaviest calibre, at a short range, is to take place before she is sent out to engage us. She is still in the dry-dock at Norfolk, and yet needs a goodly quantity of iron to complete her casing, all of which is furnished from Richmond. She has her old engines on board, and they have been made to work tolerably well. They are not expected, however, I understand, to afford anything more than a moderate velocity.

"On coming out, she must, necessarily, proceed as low down as about Sewall's Point before she can shape her course to the westward for Newport News, and this will bring her within three and a half miles of us. My present purpose is to let her get well over towards the Congress and Cumberland, off Newport News, and then to put at her with this ship and every thing else that may be on hand at the time, with a view of bringing her between the fire of those ships and these, and cutting off all retreat on her part. It is understood that she is to be assisted by the two steamers up James River, but as they cannot be made very powerful, I attach no very great consequence to this intention.

" Nothing, I think, but very close work can possibly be of service in accomplishing the destruction of the Merrimac, and even of that a great deal may be necessary. From what I gather, boarding is impracticable, as she can only be assailed in that way through the ports, of which she has, in all, but fourteen.

If I could be furnished with a couple of tugs or small steamers, to attend upon the Congress and Cumberland, in season, so as to tow these promptly into position in case of necessity, they might prove of very great service. It will be, I infer, at least a fortnight before the Merrimac will make her attempt; but in the meantime I could employ those tugs or steamers very advantageously in the way of guard vessels at night, despatch and tow vessels by day, etc., etc.,     *          *          *          *          *          *

"Your most obdt. servant,
(*Signed,*)     " L. M. GOLDSBOROUGH,
" To the Hon'ble                              " Flag Officer.
   " THE SECRETARY OF THE NAVY."

## *Extract from Letter of Capt. John Marston.*

"U. S. STEAMER ROANOKE,
"HAMPTON ROADS, February 21, 1862.

" Hon. GIDEON WELLES,
    " Secretary of the Navy, Washington, D. C.

    " SIR : &ast; &ast; &ast; By a dispatch which I received last evening from General Wool, I learn that the Merrimac will positively attack Newport News within five days, acting in conjunction with the Jamestown and Yorktown from James River, and that the attack will be made at night. I can only regret that the Roanoke should be without an engine, and has a deficiency of 180 men in her crew ; but you may be assured we shall do our best.

        " Very respectfully, your obd't. servant,

            " (*Signed*,)    JOHN MARSTON,

                " Captain and Senior Officer."

By the last extract it will be seen that, during the latter part of February and early part of March, the attack of the Merrimac was *daily expected*, and, by Mr. Fox's letter, so far from the Navy Department depending on the Congress and Cumberland to " take care" of the Merrimac, the Congress had actually been ordered away from Newport News, as a precaution, in consequence of her deficient crew.

This was exactly the period when General McClellan was preparing to fill the waters of the " lower Chesapeake" with transports crowded with troops.

---

### NOTE 3.—PAGE 16.

Col. Lecomte's remarks are noticed only on account of the inspiration under which he writes, and the associations which he has had. In the published translation of a former work of his, entitled, " The War in the United States," his account of " the Federal artillery" is thus characterized, in a foot note (p. 59), by Gen. Barry : " It would be scarcely possible to collect more errors in so small a space." He has demonstrated the possibility, however, in his account of the fortifications of Washington. Looking over the map of the defences as it is, or as it was during Col. Lecomte's service here, I find but one single one which was not primarily selected either by myself or by subordinates charged with carrying out my views in reference to the general design. That single exception was a site so prominent and so excellent that it was strange it had been thus far overlooked by us, and that its primary selection should be due to another—the late and lamented General Richardson. Some of the sites selected were examined by Gen. McClellan, and, in general, all were known and approved by him previous to commencement. That the individual works were models of engineering skill (and it is in this point of view *alone* that our critic deigns to pay us a compliment) is not pretended. As individual works they were very defective, and have required numerous alterations. The pressure was too great to admit of matured plans or elaborate construction. The *line* remains to this day essentially as it was established in the months of August and September, 1861, and though not throughout absolutely the best, perhaps, that could be selected, is so nearly so as to surprise those who, understanding the enormous difficulties of fixing such a line in so short a time, in a country so broken and covered with woods, have carefully examined it.

In another place Col. Lecomte has given additional evidence of the extraordinary talent which so astonished Gen. Barry. In reference to our ignorance concerning the topography of the Peninsula, affirmed by me in my official report, and confirmed by Gen. McClellan, he sapiently, and with a high spirit of justice doubtless, remarks, "The blame must chiefly rest upon Gen. Barnard himself, who, as commander of the engineers, was bound to procure in advance all possible information as to topography and hydrography of the country."

Col. Lecomte's business in this country was to observe the war and to study the organization, etc., of the armies of the United States. As a member of Gen. McClellan's staff he had peculiar facilities for studying the organization of the Army of the Potomac —then a type of our organizations elsewhere. Shall we impute it to ignorance that, in his three or four months of service, he did not learn that there were on the staff of that army two distinct Chiefs of Engineers—the one of engineers proper, and the other of *Topographical engineers?* that it was the province of the latter to collect the information which he specifies? This supposition seems incredible. It is, moreover, negatived by a foot-note, which he has adopted as his own to the translation of his book, by which he recognizes the existence (at the time) of a Corps of Topographical Engineers.

It was the function of the Chief of Topographical Engineers to obtain the topographical information for the intended campaign; but neither he nor any one else could do it without an intimation as to where such researches were required, and Gen. McClellan has exhibited the sources of the (worse than useless) information that he had, and has relieved everybody but himself from the blame of something worse than neglect of duty.

As to the real value, at that time, of the works for defending Washington, the following is General McClellan's testimony (p. 427):

"I regarded the defences of Washington as adequate for its protection, and that the movement of the Army of the Potomac would necessarily draw from in front of Washington the force that had previously threatened it. My mind had always been clear and distinct that the moment the army moved on any line from the lower Chesapeake, the rebels must necessarily abandon Manassas. I never doubted that a second—always *bearing in mind that the defences of Washington were complete.*"

I have made some statements elsewhere as to the degree of completeness, containing my written official opinion given Dec. 6, 1861 (in connection with this very matter), that it " would not be safe to leave Washington guarded by less than 100,000 men—that is, until we had become certain that the enemy had withdrawn from our front so far as to render his return upon it impracticable." (See Appendix.)

My argument was precisely the reverse of that above quoted from Gen. McClellan. If the enemy had 100,000 men at Manassas, and our army moved on any line from the lower Chesapeake (leaving Washington guarded by much less than 100,000 men) he would *not* abandon Manassas, but attack Washington.

---

## Note 4.—Page 19.

" Knowing that Gen. Huger could easily spare some troops to reinforce Yorktown, that he had indeed done so, and that Johnston's army of Manassas could be brought rapidly by the James and

York Rivers to the same points, I proposed to invest that town without delay.

"The accompanying map of Col. Cram, U. S. Topographical Engineers attached to Gen. Wool's staff, given to me as the result of several months' labor, indicated the feasibility of the design."

---

## NOTE 5.—PAGE 20.

Nor did the Navy Department ever undertake to reduce the batteries at Yorktown.

The following extract from the testimony of Ass't. Sec'y Fox, Admiral Goldsborough, and Major-Gen. Hitchcock, are important to a full understanding of this matter.

A letter had been addressed by me by order of Gen. McClellan to Mr. Fox concerning the Merrimac. Mr. Fox testifies:

"To this dispatch I sent the following reply:

"'NAVY DEPARTMENT, March 13, 1862.

"'The Monitor is more than a match for the Merrimac, but she may be disabled in the next encounter. I cannot advise so great a dependence upon her.

"'Burnside and Goldsborough are very strong for the Chowan River route to Norfolk, and I brought up maps, explanations, &c. It turns everything and is only 27 miles to Norfolk by two good roads. Burnside will have Newbern this week.

"'The Merrimac must go into dock for repairs. The Monitor may, and I think will destroy the Merrimac in the next fight, but this is hope, not certainty.

"'G. V. Fox,
"'Assistant Secretary.
"'MAJOR-GEN. G. B. McCLELLAN,
"'Fairfax Court House.'

"Then I got a private note from Gen. McClellan dated, 'Fairfax Court House, March 14,' in which he says:

"'From all accounts received I have such a living faith in the gallant little Monitor that I feel that we can trust her; so I have determined on the Fort Monroe movement.'

"That is all the correspondence there was with the Navy Department upon that subject. It shows that this plan of Gen. McClellan was changed between the time I arrived at Old Point Comfort, which was on the morning of the 9th of March, and the time when I got back to Washington, which, I think, was on the 12th. It was determined that the army should go by way of Fort Monroe. The Navy Department never was consulted at all, to my knowledge, in regard to anything connected with the matter. No statement was ever made to us, why they were going there beyond this. All that we were told about it is what I have read here. Admiral Golds borough was put in communication with Gen. McClellan and directed to coöperate with him; and all the force we had available was placed at the disposal of the admiral. I have no knowledge that anything that Gen. McClellan wanted in the way of attack or defence was ever neglected by our people. No complaint was ever made to the Navy Department. There was never any plan devised by the War Department that I know of, that required the navy to operate. The Secretary simply ordered the ships there to do what they could as the exigencies arose. In the private letter from which I have read, Gen. McClellan speaks of operations against Yorktown and Gloucester. But I do not think any of the army officers expected those places to be attacked by ships. Yorktown is sixty or seventy feet above the water; the vessels could not reach the batteries on the crest of the hill, and therefore they would be exposed to destruction without being able to return the fire. Admiral Goldsborough was in constant communication with Gen. McClellan, and they were very well disposed towards each other to the last moment so far as I ever knew.

"*Question.* It has been said that one reason for the failure of the Peninsula campaign was the detention of the army before the lines of Yorktown a whole month, in consequence of the navy not being able to co-operate and secure to us the free navigation of the York and James Rivers. Will you state what you know in relation to that matter?"

"*Answer.* So far as I know all the vessels that Gen. McClellan required in his operations against Yorktown, were placed at his disposal by Admiral Goldsborough. I am not aware that he ever required that we should attack Yorktown, or that it was ever expected that we should do so. All the avenues of supply to the army there were free and open as far as the army had possession.

Gen. McClellan expected the navy to neutralize the Merrimac, and I promised that it should be done, and that she should never pass Hampton Roads."

Admiral Goldsborough testifies :

" With regard to that campaign no naval authority whatever to my knowledge was ever consulted until after a considerable part of the army got down there. The whole matter was arranged here in Washington by officers of the army, as I understood. I believe they never said a word even to the Secretary of the Navy. Certainly nothing was ever said to me till the eleventh hour. Then it was that I heard that they expected the navy to coöperate with them. The Assistant Secretary of War, Mr. Watson, came down to see me in behalf, as he said, of the Secretary of War and the President of the United States. He told me of the great anxiety felt in Washington in regard to the Merrimac ; that they were apprehensive that she might get up the York River and entirely disconcert all the movements of the army. I told Mr. Watson that the President might make his mind perfectly easy about the Merrimac going up the York River ; that she never could get there, for I had ample means to prevent that. This was in the latter part of March, 1862. The army at that time was about assembling at Old Point Comfort. Gen. McClellan had not then arrived. I recollect making such observations to the Assistant Secretary of War as I think left him perfectly well satisfied that the Merrimac could never get up the York River. The plan of going up the York River was a matter decided upon here in Washington.

\*          \*          \*          \*          \*          \*

" *Question.* Were you ever requested by Gen. McClellan to perform any naval service in connection with the operations of the army that you did not perform ?

" *Answer.* No sir. I was requested to perform services in connection with the army, and every thing was done that was asked. Gen. McClellan, before coming down himself sent Col. Woodbury to consult me in regard to the best plan of attacking Yorktown. I pointed out to that officer, what I considered the best mode. A day or two afterwards Gen. McClellan sent down Gen. Barnard to consult me. I told him that I had already explained my views very fully to Col. Woodbury and repeated them to him. Some short time after that Gen. Hitchcock came down ; whether sent by anybody I don't know. He came on board my ship to consult me about the matter, and I pointed out to him what I thought the best plan, and he as well as the other two officers, seemed to agree with me perfectly. When Gen. McClellan came down, he did not go on shore the first day, but immediately came on board my ship to consult with me as to the best mode of attacking Yorktown. The approach to Richmond was to be up the York River; the approach up the James River was never mentioned."

General Hitchcock goes at great length into the merits of the plan of campaign, and into the causes which caused McDowell's corps to be retained. (Franklin's division was sent, however, and afterwards McCall's, so that on the Chickahominy Gen. McClellan had all the troops he ever counted upon having, except King's division, which was replaced by troops received from Fortress Monroe and elsewhere.) Though necessarily long, Gen. Hitchcock's testimony should be read, and most of it is introduced here.

"A military objection to the plan was his separating his army from its proper base, which was Washington, and transferring it to a point from which it could not return in case of disaster without great danger. That is a military principle which Gen. McClellan himself recognized in a communication to the President in objection to a plan of the President, as I understood. That military objection is substantially this: that in taking the army up the Peninsula Gen. McClellan made two points of defence, one the city of Washington and the other the position he assumed on the Peninsula. These two points were widely separated, and did not communicate with each other. He thus gave the enemy an opportunity of concentrating upon either of them, while it obliged the Union forces to be divided in order to secure the defence of the military point here at Washington. That, among military men, I believe, is considered to be one of the most dangerous conditions in which a body of troops can be placed. It is particularly illustrated in the history of Frederick the Great, who destroyed in succession three armies which were separated, and not in communication with each other, and gained his chief military glory from that fact. My objection to the whole of that plan was very serious, and I should on no account have acquiesced in it had I been consulted.

"When the President issued his order acquiescing in the movement proposed by Gen. McClellan, he required, as that order will show, that Washington should be left entirely secure in the opinion of all the corps commanders then there. That opinion, as appears by the report of their council, on the 13th March last, required, according to the view of three of those corps commanders, that all the forts south of the Potomac should be fully garrisoned; the forts north of the Potomac should be occupied, and in addition to that a covering force of 25,000 men. The other corps commander, Gen. Sumner, was of the opinion that 40,000 men would be sufficient to make the city secure, indicating nothing in regard to their distribution.

"There is a feature in the proceedings of that council which is very important in this connection. The council agreed to the proposed movement by way of the Peninsula, provided the rebel steamer Merrimac could be neutralized, and they were unanimous in that opinion. Gen. McClellan did not regard that part of their report, but proceeded to execute his plan while the Merrimac was still supposed to be in good condition, with a power that no one can very easily estimate. If she had not been afterwards destroyed, she might have destroyed all of the navy and all of the shipping about Fortress Monroe, and then would have been the means of destroying McClellan's army, cutting it off from supplies, and leaving it helpless. Subsequent events fortunately relieved Gen. McClellan in a great degree from the consequences of disregarding that feature in the decision of the council. The immediate consequence of disregarding that opinion of the council was, that the navy was unable to coöperate to its full extent with Gen. McClellan in reducing Gloucester Point and Yorktown, being held at Fortress Monroe to watch this single vessel the Merrimac.

"With regard to the opinion of the council as to what was required for the defence of Washington, I consider it as applying to the capital itself, to Washington, and its immediate front towards the enemy, and as not extending to the Shenandoah Valley, to Harper's Ferry, or to Baltimore. I construe the opinion of the council as requiring that all the forts in the neighborhood of Washington should be manned, and that, over and above that, there should be an army or unit of force of 25,000 men as a covering force in front of the city. I am not able to find in the public reports connected with these proceedings any evidence that this requirement of the council was complied with.

"General McClellan made a report, dated steamer Commodore,

April 1, 1862, showing a certain distribution of forces for the defence of Washington. That report enumerates 18,000 men left at Washington for the immediate defence of the capital. It speaks of the forces under Gen. Abercrombie and Gen. Geary amounting to 7,780. This report of Gen. McClellan is so miscellaneous in its mode of statement that it is difficult to determine with any accuracy the precise forces left at the various points referred to in it. It seems to count Blenker's division as a part of the force in front of Washington, and yet speaks of his design to order that division from Warrenton to Strasburgh. It was ordered from Warrenton through Strasburgh, and still further on out of this vicinity entirely into the Mountain Department. It speaks of Banks' division as if in front of Washington, and yet that division was ordered into the Valley of the Shenandoah, in consequence of the attack made by Jackson upon Shields at Winchester, so that both Banks and Blenker were removed from in front of Washington, and could not be considered as a part of the 25,000 required as a unit of force in front of the city.

" Making that deduction, I find the force in the city and the two guards, for they were little else, under Abercrombie and Geary, altogether make less than 25,000 men. I considered, therefore, that the order of the President with respect to the defence of the capital had been ' neglected,' to use his own phrase. I did not consider the force in the Shenandoah Valley as available for the immediate defence of the capital, being required for the defence of that Valley. The report made by Gen. Wadsworth to the Secretary of War on the 2d of April, which I understand is in possession of the Committee, will show the condition and character of the troops under his command. When this state of things became known to the Secretary of War, Mr. Stanton, he required Gen. Thomas and myself to make a report upon the execution of the President's order, the letter of Gen. McClellan of the 1st April, the report of Gen. Wadsworth on the 2d April, and one or two other papers connected with them, requiring us to give a distinct opinion whether Gen. McClellan had complied or not with the requirements of the order of the President. On examining those papers we were of opinion that the order of the President had not been complied with, and so reported. This report of course went to the President, and on the next day, if I mistake not, the 3d April, the President came to the War Office, and had quite a long conversation with the chiefs of the various bureaus of the War Department, the Secretary of War being present. At the conclusion of that consultation, the President himself ordered that one of the corps of the Army of the Potomac which were then in front of Washington, should be detained for the defence of the capital. The selection was left with the Secretary of War, who designated the corps commanded by Gen. McDowell. I will mention that Gen. McDowell himself was not present, and I believe knew nothing of the steps which led to his detention here until after the order was issued. As soon as General McClellan heard of this he complained of it. He wished the whole of McDowell's corps sent to him. If he could not get the whole of it, he wanted McCall's and Franklin's divisions, leaving one division only here. Failing in that, he wished particularly to have Franklin's division ordered to join him. The President again came to the War Office on the 11th April, if I mistake not, and held another conference of considerable length with the same officers as before, the chiefs of bureaus, and the Secretary of War. It was plain that the President was extremely anxious to gratify Gen. McClellan and to give him every possible support in his power, not losing sight of his imperative duty to see that this capital was sufficiently guarded. The result of that conference was, that he ordered Franklin's division to join McClellan, and it was accordingly sent down to him.

&ast;  &ast;  &ast;  &ast;  &ast;  &ast;

" *Question.* Do you understand now the movement made by General McClellan to Fortress Monroe and up the York River was in compliance with the recommendation of the council of generals commanding army corps, and held at Fairfax Court House on the 13th March last, or in violation of it ?

" *Answer.* I have considered, and do now consider that it was in violation of the recommendation of that council in two important particulars ; one particular being that portion of their report which represents the council as agreeing to the expedition by way of the Peninsula provided the rebel steamer Merrimac could first be neutralized. That very important proviso General McClellan disregarded. The other particular that he disregarded was the leaving a force for the safety of Washington. He did not leave the force which, as I have considered, the council contemplated in that report as necessary.

" *By the Chairman.*

" *Question.* On whom did the responsibility rest for the violation of those orders and the consequences that followed that violation ?

" *Answer.* I had occasion a few days since to answer a question similar to that before the court in the case of Gen. McDowell. I believe that among military men it is a settled principle that whenever a subordinate assumes to depart from a strict obedience to the orders of his superior, he takes upon himself the entire responsibility of all that follows ; and he can only protect himself from the military penalties of disobedience by some brilliant success. I have considered that Gen. McClellan was in that condition ; that in departing from the original instructions received from the President, he took upon himself the entire responsibility of that whole movement, and when subsequently the President found it necessary to detain a part of McClellan's forces in front of Washington to make good his original order, he performed an act of imperious duty, and Gen. McClellan had no right to complain of that act as an interference with his command or as tending to embarrass his operations.

" Situated as Gen. McCllelan was in front of Washington, under the orders of the President, his first duty was to comply with these orders—and having done that, then to consider whether he had sufficient force to accomplish the expedition he contemplated. If he found that he had not a sufficient force for that purpose, then he should have so represented to the President, and then the relation of the parties would have been entirely changed, and the responsibility would have been entirely with the President. But inasmuch as General McClellan did not adopt that course, but went on his expedition of his own motion, following a plan different from that of the President, he took upon himself the entire responsibility of all that followed. The President, in yielding to the plan of Gen. McClellan, put him under very explicit orders to leave Washington entirely secure, not only in his own opinion, but in the opinion of all the four commanders of corps-d'armée. These four commanders gave an opinion. As I understand the matter, Gen. McClellan did not comply with that opinion, and therein Gen. McClellan took upon himself the responsibility of all the results that grew out of his campaign."

## Note 6.—Page 20.

The Council of Corps Commanders held at Fairfax Court House, March 13, 1862, were of opinion (*vide* McClellan's Report, pp. 59 and 60) :

" I. That the enemy having retreated from Manassas to Gordonsville behind the Rappahannock and Rapidan, it is the opinion of the generals commanding army corps that the operations to be carried on will be best undertaken from Old Point Comfort, between the York and James Rivers.

" *Provided,*

" 1st. That the enemy's vessel Merrimac can be neutralized.

" 2d. That the means of transportation, sufficient for an immediate transfer of the force to its new base can be ready at Washington and Alexandria to move down the Potomac ; and

" 3d. That a naval auxiliary force can be had to silence, or aid in silencing the enemy's batteries on the York River.

" 4th. That the force to be left to cover Washington shall be such as to give an entire feeling of security for its safety from menace. (Unanimous.)

" II. If the foregoing cannot be, the army should then be moved against the enemy, behind the Rappahannock, at the earliest possible moment, and the means for reconstructing bridges, repairing railroads, and stocking them with materials sufficient for supplying the army, should at once be collected for both the Orange and Alexandria, and Aquia and Richmond Railroads. (Unanimous.)

" N. B. That with the forts on the right bank of the Potomac fully garrisoned and those on the left bank occupied, a covering force in front of the Virginia line of 25,000 men would suffice, (Keys, Heintzelman and McDowell.) A total of 40,000 men for the defence of the city would suffice. (Sumner.)"

It is to be particularly observed that, if the four conditions or provisos imposed upon the adoption of the first plan " cannot be," then " the army should be moved against the enemy behind the Rappahannock, &c."

Now the " enemy's vessel, the Merrimac" was *not* neutralized, and nothing was *established* concerning her further than that she should not be permitted to escape from Hampton Roads.

As to the second proviso, the council does not fix what it means by an " immediate transfer," but it is well known that only transportation for part of the army, at a time, could be furnished, and that three weeks were consumed in getting less than three corps to Fort Monroe.

As to the third proviso, the council define with some precision what they mean by their emphatic language " the force left to cover Washington shall be such as to give an *entire feeling of security for its safety from menace.*"

If these conditions cannot be fulfilled, the army is to be at once " moved against the enemy behind the Rappahannock." The conditions were not fulfilled, nay more, they were completely disregarded, and in his conduct in thus disregarding the counsels of others as to the safety of Washington, and leading his army into a region, of which he had no knowledge, Gen. McClellan exhibited at least infatuation and levity of conduct, not to speak of the graver aspect of his course as a positive disobedience of orders.

## Note 7.—Page 23.

The following English criticism may properly find place here. (*United Service Magazine*, February, 1864) :

" As regards the value of the plan, in a merely military point of view, three faults may be enumerated : 1st. It was too rash. 2d. It violated the principles of war. 3d. Its application was too timid.

" 1st. An army of 130,000 volunteers should not be moved about as if it were a single division.

"2d. The choice of Fortress Monroe, as a secondary basis, involved the necessity of leaving Washington, or the fixed basis, to be threatened, morally at least, by the enemy. The communications also between these two places were open to an attack from the Merrimac, an iron-plated ship, which lay at Norfolk on the south side of Hampton Roads.

" The first movement to Fortress Monroe was the stride of a giant. The second, in the direction of Richmond, was that of a dwarf. When the army arrived in front of the lines at Yorktown, it numbered, probably, 100,000 men, and here there was no timid President to interfere with the command ; nevertheless McClellan suffered himself to be stopped in the middle of an offensive campaign by Magruder and 12,000 men. His previous information, which was afterwards found to be incorrect, had stated this number at 20,000, and Magruder made such skilful dispositions as effectually completed ·the deception. But a general who, as Napoleon used to say, knows his trade, will seldom be deceived. Why did he not take means to ascertain the truth? Supposing, however, that his previous information had been correct, he should not have wasted his time waiting for McDowell when every moment of it was precious. But every hour's delay after he had heard of that general's retention, created eighty chances to one against his ultimate success. The hour of his arrival in front of the lines should have been the hour of his attack upon them. Two overwhelming masses, to which life and energy had been communicated, should have been hurled on separate points. Magruder not only defeated but destroyed! The morale of the Federal army raised! The result of the campaign, although it might not have been decisive, would have been more honorable."

## Note 8.—Page 25.

The Prince de Joinville alludes as follows to the route taken:

"On May 16th" (the Prince was with head-quarters) "we reached the White House, etc.      *       *       *       *       *

"At White House the Pamunkey ceases to be navigable. The York River Railroad, which unites Richmond with this river, crosses it at this point by a bridge, which the enemy had destroyed, and then runs in almost a straight line to the Virginian capital. This road had been scarcely injured. Having neither embankments nor viaducts it was not easy to destroy it. A few rails only had been removed, and were soon replaced; all the rolling stock had been run off, *but the Federal army had locomotives and cars on board of its transports.* The whole flotilla was unloaded at White House, where a vast depot was established under the protection of the gunboats, and all the bustle of a seaport soon became visible. The army recommenced its march to Richmond, following the line of the railway, which was to be the vital artery of its operations."

## NOTE 9.—PAGE 28.

General Heintzelman testifies as follows (pp. 351 and 352, Report of Committee on the Conduct of the War) :

" As soon as I had found the attack was serious, I had sent an officer over to inform Gen. Sumner and Gen. McClellan. Gen. McClellan at once ordered Gen. Sumner to cross his troops over the Chickahominy. However, Gen. Sumner, as soon as he had heard the firing, and without waiting for orders, had put his troops under arms and marched them out of camp, thus saving an hour or so, which was of great service to us. There was one brigade of Gen. Casey's division, under Gen. Naglee, on our extreme right, that held its position pretty well. The centre gave way, and fell back some distance. We succeeded in rallying them and repulsed the enemy. My right held its ground until some time after dark, when it fell back and joined us in the field-works we had thrown up a little west of the Chickahominy. In the night I got a telegram from Gen. McClellan that he wanted to see me at the railroad station on the other side of the Chickahominy. I got on a locomotive and went down there and saw him. I told him what had occurred and what we could do. He said that he relied upon my holding the position we then occupied, and that he would either spend that night with Gen. Sumner, or come over the next morning to keep rank off me, as he said Gen. Sumner ranked me. When I got back I got a note from Gen. Sumner, saying that from all he could learn he expected to be attacked with overwhelming force in the morning, and wanted me to assist him. I replied that any aid I could give him he should have.

" In the morning I went to the front, and had not been there long before I heard firing in the direction of Gen. Sumner's forces. I had the half of Gen. Hooker's division there ; the other half was at Bottom's Bridge. I immediately sent that half division forward in the direction of the firing. They soon met the enemy, who were repulsed by Gen. Sumner's troops and mine. The whole affair was over in a very short time.

" About two o'clock in the afternoon Gen. McClellan came over to my headquarters and congratulated me on our success ; and said that he had relied upon my doing what I had promised him."

General Sumner testifies (pp. 362 and 363):

" On reaching Fair Oaks I was met by Gen. Couch, who told me that he had been separated by the enemy from the rest of the army, and was expecting an attack every moment. I formed this division of Sedgwick together with Couch's troops, assuming command of the whole as quickly as possible, with a battery of artillery between the two divisions. Before the formation was completed the enemy made a ferocious attack on my centre, evidently with the expectation of getting possession of my battery. My forces were formed in two lines, nearly at right angles. I had six regiments in hand on the left of the battery. After sustaining a very severe fire for some time, those six regiments charged directly into the woods, crossing a broken-down fence in doing so. The enemy then fled, and the action was over for that day. During that night, Saturday night, I succeeded in getting up Richardson's division and formed it parallel with the railroad. About $7\frac{1}{2}$ o'clock on Sunday morning the troops became engaged on the railroad. It is not exactly certain which party fired first. A very severe fight continued then for the space of three or four hours, in which I lost many valuable officers and men; the enemy were then entirely routed, and fled. There was fighting on the same day on my left by a portion of Gen. Heintzelman's troops, but that was at such a distance that I have myself no knowledge of the circumstances. There was no communication at that time between us.

   *    *    *    *    *    *

 " *Question.* Who had the command at the battle of Fair Oaks, or Seven Pines? They are the same thing under those two names, I understand.

 " *Answer.* No, sir, they were two distinct places. The battle in which I commanded on Saturday and Sunday was at Fair Oaks. The battle of Seven Pines was a separate battle some miles from Fair Oaks. Gen. Heintzelman was in command at Seven Pines."

 " *Question.* Where was Gen. McClellan during those battles?

 " *Answer.* Gen. McClellan came over to me at Fair Oaks about 12 o'clock on Sunday. The action of Sunday had then ceased. I asked him at once if he had any orders to give. He said no; that he had no changes to make; that he was satisfied with what had been done."

 So incoherent was the whole affair, that Gen. Sumner states that the battle of the Seven Pines was " a separate battle" from that at which he commanded (" Fair Oaks"). He is mistaken, however, in his assertion that it was " several miles" from Fair Oaks; it was scarcely more than a mile.

The railroad station on the other side "of the Chickahominy" at which Gen. Heintzelman had his interview with Gen. McClellan on Saturday night, was just about seven miles by railroad from the two fields, and about 7.30 Sunday morning the fighting was resumed at Fair Oaks, and a " severe fight continued there for the space of three or four hours." Gen. McClellan made his presence on the field known to Gen. Sumner at 12 M. and to Gen. Heintzelman at 2 P. M. He had told Gen. Heintzelman that he would be on the field the same night or " the next morning," to " keep rank off him" (Heintzelman). It would appear, therefore, that, failing to notify Heintzelman that he was to be under the orders of Sumner—positively encouraging him to feel himself independent of Sumner—he failed to appear himself, and left the two generals to do their own fighting " on their own hook."

<hr/>

NOTE 9½.—PAGE 28.

In reference to this paragraph, it is proper to say that the way of getting the right wing over the Chickahominy (in other words of " uniting the two wings of the army") in time to take part in the battle, " make a vigorous pursuit," or to do whatever else the occasion might require, was the *one theme* in the minds of all, at Headquarters as elsewhere. The bridges over the river had been ordered the night before, and Col. Alexander had spent the whole night in bridging the numerous ditches intersecting the bottom lands, all for this single object. Gen. Smith's division had been ordered down to the " New Bridge," and Brook's brigade was waiting at the bridge for the order to pass.

I have stated in my official report (p. 35) that the " New Bridge was passable" for all arms at 8.15 A. M.; that a few hours later I found the bottom lands so completely overflowed that, while the enemy held the commanding heights in front with artillery, I did not think the passage practicable; and that at that moment I was utterly ignorant of the condition of affairs on the other side. The preceding evening had brought us gloomy accounts of our situation. The battle had been renewed in the morning, and was going on. I knew nothing whether it was with success or with additional disaster to us.   Now the time of this report from me was actually about (somewhat preceding) that of the final repulse of the rebels by Gen. Sumner.   It was the very time at which to decide to take advantage of our victory to sweep the hostile forces from the heights facing " New Bridge," and to bring over our right wing—" unite" it to the left, and " make a vigorous pursuit," etc.

---

## Note 10.—Page 32.

The only bridges existing might have been seized by the enemy simultaneously with his attack, as pointed out in the following extracts :

" The left cannot be turned, being protected by the impenetrable morasses of White Oak Swamp ; but the right might be surrounded. At this very moment, indeed, a strong Confederate column is moving in that direction.   If it succeeded in getting between Bottom's Bridge and the Federal troops who are fighting at Savage's Station, the whole left wing is lost.   It will have no retreat left, and must be overwhelmed.   But exactly at this moment (6 o'clock P. M.) new actors came upon the stage."—(*Prince de Joinville.*)

" Had the attack which Sumner met and repulsed been made simultaneously with the assault in front, a single battalion, nay, a single company, could have seized and destroyed " Sumner's Upper Bridge," the only one, as before remarked, then passable.   Sumner would consequently have been unable to take part in the battle, and our left wing would have been taken in flank, and, in all probability, defeated.—(" *The Peninsular Campaign," Atlantic Monthly, March,* 1864.)

---

## Note 11.—Page 32.

A sentence in the President's dispatch of this period (May 24th), " I wish you to move cautiously and safely," is italicized by Gen. McClellan as approving of and justifying the astonishingly dilatory proceedings intended to be considered " cautious" and " safe."   This was while Heintzelman and Keyes were for a whole week lying in their remarkably " safe" positions.

## Note 12.—Page 36.

The following is Gen. McClellan's testimony, pp. 432–33 (1) :

*Question.*—" When were those bridges completed, or were they ever completed ?"

*Answer.* " The most important ones were completed, I should think, about the 20th of May—not far from then."

*Question.* " After the completion of the bridges, why was not the attempt made to drive the enemy from that position ?"

*Answer.* " The main causes of the delay were, I think, the condition of the ground and the necessity for finishing the defensive works regarded as necessary for the safety of the army should it meet with a disaster in the attack."

*Question.* " At what point were the defensive works to which you refer ?"

*Answer.* " They were mainly in the vicinity of the battle-field of Fair Oaks, and then to the right of that, looking to the position of the enemy at New Bridge. The affair of the 25th of June was the beginning of the operations against the enemy. I had expected to attack the position in rear of New Bridge by the 26th or 27th of June, but was prevented by the series of occurrences known as the seven days' battle."

The " defensive works" were to be completed, as per Report (p. 21), June 21. The " condition of the ground" was good enough at any time after those dates.

## Note 13.—Page 39.

Magruder's language as quoted by Pollard, is :

" Had McClellan massed his whole force in column, and advanced it against any point of our line of battle, as was done at Austerlitz, under similar circumstances, by the greatest captain of any age, though the head of the column would have suffered greatly, its momentum would have insured him success, and the occupation of our works about Richmond, and consequently of the city, might have been his reward."

Pollard, it is true, attempts to refute Magruder, and says that by 12 M. of Friday (June 27) the communications of Lee's main body with Richmond were re-established by the possession of the New Bridge. But the attack described by Magruder should have been made by daylight on Friday. Whether at that hour, or later, was immaterial, however, so far as the isolation of Lee was concerned, for part of our operation would have been to occupy the heights from Dr. Garnett's house to opposite Mechanicsville with artillery. Lee could not have repassed the Chickahominy without great delays and disastrous losses, and time would have been acquired for all that Magruder describes.

---

## Note 14.—Page 40.

Mr. Hiram Ketcham of New York has made a praiseworthy effort to illustrate Gen. McClellan's military exploits; in doing which he has apparently considered it necessary to his purpose to convict me of baseness of conduct and of being actuated by dishonorable motives. He finds it "melancholy to think that men, who never lack courage in the field of battle, should ever fail to speak their honest conviction where they have reason to suppose their undisguised convictions will give offence to those in power."

He sees "a melancholy example of this truth in the case of Gen. Barnard," and does not hesitate to affirm that I "knew what kind of testimony the Committee wanted," and to insinuate that I shaped it accordingly (I was unconscious that such a Committee yet existed when I wrote the report which constitutes the bulk of my "testimony.")

I should not have noticed this "Heraclitus" among military critics, this "melancholy" libeler of the moral character of others, and sorry apologist of Gen. McClellan, but for a letter to him of F. J. Porter, written to "bear cheerful testimony to the accuracy of his statements in reviewing the operations of this campaign, and to the soundness of his "conclusions."

In this letter the writer says, "But what induced me to address this note to you at this time is your recent review of the battle of Gaines' Mill. Our forces which amounted to 32,000 were under my command in that battle. The force of the enemy brought against us was more than double our number. If, in this battle, I had been reinforced in time with 15,000 fresh troops, the enemy who was repulsed three times would have been finally driven back and the battle won on our side."

Whatever the above "cheerful testimony" may be, in other

respects, it is a "stunner" indeed in its bearings upon the general-ship of his Chief. Fighting a decisive battle with 32,000 men against double numbers of an enemy who employed the bulk of his army in the attack, leaving between us and Richmond only just enough troops to keep up a show of force, while nearly 70,000 of our men lay idle a few miles distant, witnesses almost of the battle —it becomes evident to the dullest comprehension that (in F. J. Porter's words) "all we wanted to insure success before Richmond was the reinforcements which had been repeatedly called for by Gen. McClellan, and which by a vigorous and prompt effort could have been supplied."

---

### NOTE 15.—PAGE 42.

Pollard's "Second Year of the War" has the following para-graph:

"The assault of the enemy's works near Gaines' Mill is a memor-able part of the engagement of Friday, and the display of fortitude, as well as quick and dashing gallantry of our troops on that occa-sion, takes its place by the side of the most glorious exploits of the war. Gen. A. P. Hill had made the first assault upon the lines of the enemy's intrenchments near Gaines Mill. A fierce struggle had ensued between his division and the garrison of the line of de-fence. Repeated charges were made by Hill's troops, but the formidable character of the works, and murderous volleys from the artillery covering them, kept our troops in check."

    \*        \*        \*        \*        \*        \*

"The works carried by our noble troops would have been in-vincible to the bayonet, had they been garrisoned by men less dastardly than the Yankees. All had been done on our side with the bullet and the bayonet. For four hours had our inferior force, unaided by a single piece of artillery, withstood over 30,000, assisted by 26 pieces of artillery."

The above quotations are made in order to contradict their auda-cious misrepresentations.

The battle of "Gaines' Mill" was fought on unfortified ground, all our fortifications being guarded by the 70,000 men on the other side of the river. There was not a defensive work of any kind on that side of the Chickahominy, and as to the "inferior force" of the rebels, there were by Pollard's own statements present, the corps of Jackson estimated at 35,000; the corps of Longstreet, consisting of his own division and that of D. H. Hill; the corps of A. P. Hill ("about 14,000 men"—Pollard) and the troops of Brig.-Gen. Branch (number unknown). The number of 65,000, given afterwards in the Richmond papers, is fully made up in the above organizations. Porter's corps (including McCall) numbered about 27,000; it was reinforced to about 35,000, but Slocum's division, the only reinforcement that took part in the battle, kept on its legs from 7 A. M., did not get into action until 3.30 P. M.

Concerning the manner in which reinforcements were actually furnished to Porter, the following extract is made from Gen. Franklin's testimony, showing how the only body of men that actually did reach Porter in time to take part in the battle, was handled:

"At 7 o'clock in the morning of that day I was ordered to send Gen. Slocum's division to assist Gen. Porter. This order was countermanded about 9 o'clock, after a part of the division had crossed the Chickahominy; the division was then sent to its old position. I was again ordered about 2 o'clock in the afternoon to send it to the assistance of Gen. Porter. It did go over and was severely engaged, losing nearly 2,000 men.

"*Question.* Do you know why the order for Slocum's division to move forward was countermanded?

"*Answer.* The order to send the division over was signed by Col. Colburn, and I sent back some word, I do not remember what. Gen. Marcy answered that he hardly supposed the general commanding could have intended to send the division over; that there must have been some mistake about it, he thought. Then about 9 o'clock, perhaps nearly 10, the order was countermanded, the order countermanding coming from Gen. McClellan, although I do not remember who signed it. What was the reason for ordering the division back I do not know."

At 5 P.M., when the fortunes of the day *had become desperate*, the brigades of French and Meagher were ordered over, arriving, as might be supposed, too late to render any important service; indeed, I heard at the time, that the shouts of Meagher's men caused our troops in front to believe the rebels had got in their rear, and thus increased the disorder."

### NOTE 16.—PAGE 43.

Pollard describes the works on each side of the railroad as " turn-ing out to be an immense embrasured fortification, extending for hundreds of yards on either side of the track."

As these works were not taken by " assault " from the " dastardly Yankees," he has no reason for the exaggeration, or rather falsehood used in reference to the imaginary " intrenchments near Gaines' Mill ;" nor are the words used a very great exaggeration of the truth.   Their " defensive works," though styled by Gen. McClellan " slight earthworks," were heavier works than those at Manassas and Centreville, which he has, with another object, characterized as " strong lines of intrenchments," " heavy earth-works," etc.

### NOTE 17.—PAGE 43.

General Franklin testifies as follows :

" *Question.* If there was a necessity to keep a portion of our troops on the left bank to do that, ought there not to have been communications opened from the one bank to the other, so that the two wings could have been united without delay ?

" *Answer.* That was impossible, as the land lay then, without whipping the enemy at Old Tavern, opposite New Bridge.

" *Question.* In your judgment should not the enemy have been driven from that position instead of being allowed to remain there ?

" *Answer.* They should have been ; and I think that ought to have been done by concentrating the whole army on the same side of the river before making the attack.   I think the whole of Fitz-John Porter's command ought to have been withdrawn to the right bank of the river on the night of the 26th of June, instead of fight-ing where they did the next day."

### NOTE 18.—PAGE 44.

In Gen. McClellan's self-satisfied and self-laudatory report of June 15th, the battle of Gaines' Mill and the holding of the enemy " at bay," were but necessary incidents to the " changing of base" to the James, and he sends Gen. Woodbury on the morning of the 28th " to increase the number of bridges" over the White Oak Swamp, as if *some had already been made*. *All* the bridges and passages of the White Oak Swamp had long been, as Gen. McClellan well knew, destroyed and obstructed, and when Gen. Woodbury arrived at White Oak Swamp Bridge, on the morning of the 28th, he found Gen. Peck still engaged *in increasing the obstructions.* The confusion of ideas between retreating to the James and "taking Richmond" pervades all the statements in relation to this period. In answer to one question he tells the Committee on the Conduct of the War that the battle of Gaines' Mill enabled him "to withdraw the army and its material;" and in another he tells them that the retreat to the James was only "a contingency he thought of. But my impression is, that up to the time of the battle of Gaines' Mill, I still hoped that we should be able to hold our own."

In his dispatch to the Secretary of War, of June 28th, 12.20 A.M. (p. 131), the General says : " Had I 20,000, or even 10,000, fresh troops to use to-morrow, I could take Richmond. * * * If, at this instant, I could dispose of 10,000 fresh men, I could gain the victory to-morrow." Quite likely that he could, even *without the additional men ;* that is, that an able commander could have done so. But, after having previously stated that his enemy was nearly double his own force in numbers—that Richmond was defended by strong works—this assertion on the very heels of a disastrous defeat! Let the reader, even though he has been one of those who have laid all the blame of the disastrous failure of Gen. McClellan's campaign on the administration, and has vilified it for putting on the shelf its "ablest" commander, attentively read the dispatches published in this Report, and say what confidence any administration could, at this period, have in their author. The dispatch just quoted from, winds up by telling the Secretary of War, " You have done your best to sacrifice this army!"

---

### Note 19.—Page 45.

The following extracts from the testimony of Generals Sumner, Heintzelman, Franklin, and McCall are given in this connection. Gen. Franklin's story is very brief, but pertinent :

" *Not being able to communicate with head-quarters* I determined to evacuate the position (*i. e.,* at White Oak Swamp Bridge) at 10 o'clock at night, and fall back to the James River. Before evacuating I sent word to Gen. Heintzelman that I was about to leave."

*Sumner.* "That action also closed at dark. About 8 o'clock in the evening, while we were collecting the wounded and dead, Gen. Seymour came to me and told me that Gen. Franklin had retreated, and that Gen. Heintzelman was preparing to follow him. I had received no orders to retreat, and should not have retreated if I had not received this information. But finding myself left with my corps entirely unsupported, I felt compelled to fall back with the rest of the army to Malvern. I accordingly fell back and reported at day-light the next morning to Gen. McClellan on the James River. He told me that he had intended that the army should have held on where they were the day before, and that no orders had been sent to retreat; but as the rest of the army had fallen back, he was very glad I had done so. The next morning the troops were placed in position by direction of Gen. McClellan, under the immediate orders of the Engineer officers. The action at Malvern commenced on the left about 10 o'clock in the morning. Gen. McClellan had deemed it necessary to go down to Harrison's Landing to determine on the point to which the troops were to retire. I therefore found myself, by virtue of my seniority of rank, in command of the army, without having been invested formally with that command, or having received any instructions in relation to it."

*Heintzelman.* "About that time it got to be dusk and soon after that the firing ceased, except some little cannonading. I met three of Gen. McClellan's aides, and by one of them I had sent word how we were situated and what I thought could be done. I thought we could not hold our position, but would have to fall back. About 8 or 9 o'clock that night an officer came to me and told me that Gen. Franklin had fallen back from White Oak Swamp Bridge. I could not believe it, because that at once gave the enemy a chance to cut us off. After a while Gen. Seymour of the Pennsylvania Reserves came to me and told me the same thing. I asked him if he was sent to inform me, and he said he was not. I then said that was no authority for me and that I could not fall back. Gen. Slocum wanted me to fall back. I said that I was ordered to hold the position and must obey orders; that I had sent to head-quarters to report the condition of affairs, and expected to get an answer. I sent an aide to learn the facts. He came back and reported that Gen. Franklin had actually fallen back, and the enemy were repairing the bridge and would soon be over. I then made arrangements to fall back. I went to Gen. Sumner's head-quarters and got him to write a note to Gen. McClellan and state to him what had occurred."

*McCall.* "To McCall's division was assigned by order of the General-in-Chief (through Gen. Porter) a position a short distance in front of the point, where the line of march turned abruptly from the Newmarket road towards the river. I accordingly formed my divisions in two lines crossing at right angles the Newmarket road, and in front of the Turkey Bridge or Quaker road leading to the river, and along which the trains were then moving. Sumner's position was at some distance to the left of mine and somewhat retired; Hooker was on Sumner's left and slightly advanced; Kearney was on the opposite side of the road and consequently on my right; there was more or less interval between each two. The Confederate forces advanced from Richmond down the Newmarket road, Lee's object being to cut or break through the Union army at this point. Had he succeeded in doing so, he could have seized and strongly occupied the only two approaches to James River and then the left wing of our army (Heintzelman's and Franklin's corps) would inevitably have been cut off from McClellan, and the right wing would have been taken in rear on its march. That this was Lee's object, as it was his expectation to accomplish it, is established by the declaration of Gen. Longstreet, that, if McCall's division had not fought as well as it did, they would have captured the Federal army. (See Surgeon Marsh's testimony herewith.) And from the disposition of Lee's forces it necessarily followed that the brunt of the attack would be on my position. It was so; and to my division, which had been fighting and marching for four days and nights without rest for a single night, it was indeed a desperate affair. My division, with the exception of an unimportant reinforcement, had fought the battle of Mechanicsville single-handed, on the 26th, and had inflicted on Lee the only defeat the Confederates acknowledged they sustained in front of Richmond; their own accounts admitting they were repulsed at every point with unparalleled loss. On the 27th my division fought again at Gaines' Mill, and having lost heavily in the last battle, they were now reduced to about 6,000 men. On the 30th, at Newmarket Cross Roads, the attack was made on my division by Longstreet and A. P. Hill's division, crack troops, and about 18,000 strong. For some time my division alone was engaged, several attempts having been made to find a weak point in my line.

&ast;          &ast;          &ast;          &ast;          &ast;          &ast;

" Had my division been routed, the march of the Federal army would certainly have been seriously interrupted by Lee forcing his masses into the interval. (See Gen. Porter's statement herewith.) When I was surrounded and taken prisoner, I was conducted at once to Lee's head-quarters. Here Longstreet told me they had 70,000 men bearing on that point, all of whom would arrive before midnight; and had he succeeded in forcing McClellan's column of march, they would have been thrust in between the right and left wings of the Federal army. Now, under this very probable contingency, had I not held my position, (see Gen. Porter's report herewith,) the state of affairs in the left wing of McClellan's army would have been critical indeed; but Lee was checked (as Longstreet admitted) by my division (see Surgeon Marsh's report herewith) and the divisions in the rear, together with the Pennsylvania Reserves, and others moved on during the night and joined McClellan at Malvern Hill before daylight.'

------------------------

NOTE 20.—PAGE 46.

The " rout of McCall's division," refuted by Gen. McCall himself has been a subject of controversy. That the division contributed most essentially to the saving of the army, and that it was in no proper sense of the word " routed," is maintained, and I think, successfully by that general.

" It was *very* late at night," indeed, before it was known at head-quarters that any disaster had taken place with McCall—that he himself was wounded—that Meade was wounded, Simmons killed, and Seymour's brigade dispersed and himself missing. The affair was over at dark and the distance from Dew's house, where (after dark) was Gen. McClellan, about three miles. Yet such was the efficiency of the command and of the staff arrangements, that an event upon which hinged the fortunes of the next day and the fate of the army, was not known until " very late at night," nor even then was " the true position of affairs" at all understood. The army (as stated elsewhere) was saved by the independent action of the corps commanders.

---

### NOTE 21.—PAGE 46.

The commanding general in his evidence before the Committee on the Conduct of the War is strangely oblivious of a six hours' journey made on a day of battle.

" *Question.* At what point or points were you from the time you left the field until you returned ?

"*Answer.* I was at head-quarters, near Haxall's house.

" *Question.* Were you down to the river or on board the gunboats during any part of that day, between the time you left the field and your return to it ?

"*Answer.* I do not remember; it is possible I may have been, as my camp was directly on the river."

In the report, however, (p. 138) it is stated that after making the " entire circuit of the position, I returned to Haxall's, whence I went with Capt. Rodgers to select the final location for the army and its depots," and that he "returned to Malvern before the serious fighting commenced."

On the 26th June we have seen that the enemy was so discourteous as to frustrate our " final advance," decided upon for that day, by " attacking our right in strong force" at 3½ P. M. of same day. On this memorable day of Malvern he is far from being so disobliging, since he waits until after 5 P. M. for the general's return to commence his " serious fighting."

The following is Gen. Heintzelman's account :

" After some time I rode over to Malvern Hill, and found Gen. McClellan, who had just got information of what was going on" (he alludes to the falling back of the army from Glendale and White Oak Swamps, of which I have quoted his account in Note 16.) " He directed me to go and find Gen. Porter and Gen. Barnard, his chief engineer, and they would point out the ground on Malvern Hill we could occupy. I found them, but it was so dark that we could not do anything. It was half past one o'clock in the morning then. I laid down and slept a little while. At daylight I called those generals, and they went out to see where we could be posted.

After an hour or more they came back and pointed out the direction very indefinitely. A few minutes after Gen. McClellan arrived. I joined him and we went round, and he pointed out the position for Gen. Porter's corps and told me where to post mine. I left staff-officers to post the troops, and went around and left Gen. McClellan at his camp on James River. About 10 o'clock that day the enemy commenced an attack with artillery. We replied to them when, after a while, it ceased. Not long after it commenced again. They sent some infantry up. That attack was repulsed and ceased. Late in the afternoon they made their grand attack on our extreme left. That lasted until some time after night. We gave them a very thorough repulse. Late in the afternoon Gen. Porter sent to Gen. Sumner for a brigade and battery. Gen. Sumner turned to me and asked me what I thought of it. I said, ' by all means furnish it ; if we are beaten, we may as well be defeated at one place as at another.' I also sent a brigade and a battery, and the consequence was we gave them that terrible defeat so that they did not follow us the next day.

" *Question.* Where was Gen. McClellan during that fight ?

" *Answer.* He was down at his head-quarters on the James River. He came up some time late in the afternoon. Gen. Sumner told one of his aides that he had sent up, that he intended to mass his troops, unless he gave orders to the contrary. That was made known to Gen. McClellan and he sent up orders not to move the troops. He came up and was with Gen. Porter about half an hour."

In reference to the battle of Malvern, Gen. McClellan states (p. 138) :

" Gen. Barnard then received full instructions for posting the troops as they arrived," and Gen. Heintzelman testifies above, " that those generals, (Porter and Barnard,) after making a tour of the field," came back and " pointed out the direction very indefinitely."

I knew nothing about Gen. Porter in this connection, but I know that I returned, as stated by Gen. Heintzelman, and " pointed out" to him the direction, and described as well as I could the whereabouts of a position for him—it being out of my power at that moment to do anything more. Excepting an orderly I was *alone.* My acting *aide-de-camp,* Lieut. Abbot, had gone down to " Haxall's" sick—my adjutant, Lieut. Hall, had been taken from me by Gen.

Marcy forty-eight hours before, without any intimation to me, and I had not seen him the previous day or night. Col. Alexander, Lieut. Comstock, and Lieut. Farquhar had been sent away on a reconnoissance and had not since reported. I could not lead Gen. Heintzelman's corps to its position, but desirous of getting it out of the way (as the other corps were now rapidly crowding in) indicated the road to take, and described as definitely as possible an approximate position; I sent a pressing request to head-quarters for aides, and returned to an examination of the field, presuming Gen. Heintzelman would move his corps in the direction I indicated, and that I should place it more "definitely" afterwards.

It seems that Gen. McClellan gave orders to me to "post the troops," went to Haxall's, and gave exactly the same order to Gen. Humphrey, without notifying him or me of the other's orders—then went into the field and (according to Gen. Heintzelman's account) *posted the troops himself.**

In my report (p. 42) I have done injustice to Gen. Humphreys in speaking of him merely as an assistant. I was not aware that he had independent orders, nor that the officers who accompanied him had been primarily directed to report *to him,* and not to me. As stated in my report, the execution of the "posting" was done by others after I left that part of the line (the relative positions of the different corps having been agreed on between us) and was done under direction of Gen. Humphreys. The giving of independent orders to Gen. Humphreys and myself, and the subsequent direct orders to corps commanders, and the ignorance, in which Gen. Sumner was left as to the positions of the troops, when, by Gen. McClellan's departure, the command of the whole army devolved upon him (see Note 19) are all characteristic.

---

## Note 22.—Page 47.

Inapt to confirm and take advantage of an existing superiority in the morale of his army, as we have seen Gen. McClellan to be at Yorktown, to seize a moment of victory and of very complete demoralization in the enemy's ranks after the battle of Fair Oaks, it be-

---

* Gen. McClellan also states in his evidence before the Committee on the Conduct of the War: "I selected the positions in a general way.    *    *    * *indicating to the different commanders* the approximate positions they were to occupy."

comes almost amusing to read the following, from his testimony before the Committee on the Conduct of the War:

"*Question.* Will you state in what you consider your chances for success would have been greater with the addition of 20,000 men to the number which you had at Harrison's Landing, than they were when you were in front of Richmond, and before Jackson had formed a junction with the rest of the rebel forces?

"*Answer.* I should have counted upon the effect of the battles which had just taken place upon the enemy. We had then strong reason to believe that the enemy's losses had been very much heavier than our own, and that portions of his army were very much demoralized, especially after the battle of Malvern Hill."

A battle-field from which we made a precipitate retreat, leaving our dead and wounded in the hands of the enemy, was not a matter to cause great elation on our side, nor seriously to demoralize our enemy; and as for losses, whatever they might have been to the enemy, Gen. McClellan estimates his numbers at 20,000 men. It is almost perverting language to use it seriously as used in the above quotation. Our own army, if not demoralized, had lost all that self-confidence—that sense of invincibility, which makes, when it exists, the moral strength of an army. It had not the "elan" of victory, for it knew not what victory was. After four months of hardship, unrelieved by any brilliant successes—always in its battles (even at Williamsburg) fighting on the defensive — driven at length from Richmond, and barely succeeding in each combat on its retreat in holding its own, while abandoning dead and wounded and losing heavily in that of which the loss so much touches the soldier's pride—artillery—the army was certainly disheartened, and in the higher ranks, confidence in the commander was wanting.

To appreciate the state of feeling in the rebel army (whether its "losses" had been "heavier" than our own or not), let the circumstances be considered. Hardly more than one month before a relative of Jeff Davis wrote: "When I think of the dark gloom that now hovers over our country, I am ready to sink with despair. * * * Uncle Jeff thinks we had better go to a safer place than Richmond." * * * * * *

And now, at this moment of which we write, the great source of unhappiness was that Gen. McClellan's army had been *permitted to escape at all.*

Pollard ("Second Year of the War"), page 75:

"The glory and fruits of our victory may have been seriously diminished by the grave mishap or fault by which the enemy was permitted to leave his camp on the south side of the Chickahominy, in an open country, and to plunge into the dense cover of wood and swamp, when the best portion of a whole week was consumed in hunting him and finding out his new position, only in time to attack him under the uncertainty and disadvantage of the darkness of night.

" But the successes achieved in the series of engagements which had already occurred were not to be lightly esteemed, or to be depreciated, because of the errors which, if they had not occurred, would have made our victory more glorious and complete. The seige of Richmond had been raised ; an army of 150,000 men had been pushed from their strongholds and fortifications and put to flight; we had enjoyed the eclat of an almost daily succession of victories; we had gathered an immense spoil in stores, provisions, and artillery ; we had demolished and dispersed, if we had not succeeded in annihilating, an army which had every resource that could be summoned to its assistance, every possible addition to numbers within the reach of the Yankee government, and every material condition of success to ensure for it the great prize of the capital of the Confederacy, which was now, as far as human judgment could determine, irretrievably lost to them, and secure in the protection of a victorious army."

The dashing, fearless, and enterprising army which Lee brought against Pope is the most perfect illustration of "the effects of the battles which had just taken place upon the enemy ;" and it was against such a body of men, numbering 200,000 (according to his own estimates), that Gen. McClellan was going to march with 120,000 men, counting upon the demoralization produced ("especially ") by Malvern Hill !

It was, as we all know, the habit of Napoleon to estimate in numbers the chances for and against success in his plans of campaign. Gen. McClellan, however, quite exceeds Napoleon in accuracy of calculation. From an enemy 200,000 strong, "very much demoralized" (as we know) by "the battle of Malvern Hill," we, with 120,000 men, "can take Richmond if we have *but half a chance.*"— (Dispatch of July 12, 1862.)

## Note 23, to Appendix, page 51.

It may be doubted whether this is a fair exhibition of Gen. McClellan's plan; whether such a scheme could really have been soberly entertained.

Urbanna is 50 miles in a straight line from Richmond. Across the route lay the "Dragon Swamp" (head of the Piankatank River), the two formidable rivers, the Matapony and Pamunkey, and the well-known Chickahominy.

From Fredericksburg to Richmond is, in a straight line, but about 50 miles; from Manassas Junction to Richmond 80 miles, or by railroad 120 miles. To collect transports for 35,000 or 40,000 men; to embark that number, move to Urbanna, land that force, with its artillery, horses, and supplies, force the passage of the Piankatank, the two great rivers mentioned, and the Chickahominy, before the enemy could move his forces at Fredericksburg and Manassas, 50, 80, and 120 miles, with railroads all the way, is truly an incredible conception. Here, however, is Gen. McClellan's testimony:

"*Question.* Did you anticipate that that movement could be made without the knowledge of the rebels, and in such a manner as to enable you to cut off or intercept their retreat from Manassas to Centreville?

"*Answer.* I do not think that we could entirely intercept their retreat to Richmond, but the chances were that if this movement was fairly started, before they were aware of it, we could fight them in front of Richmond to their disadvantage, before they could get all their troops in hand.

"*Question.* Do you mean by that that you expected to intercept their retreat to Richmond in such a manner as to divide their forces, leaving a part of it on this side of the point where you intercept their communications, and then fight the balance of it at Richmond?

"*Answer.* In reply to that I can only repeat that I hoped, if proper secrecy was observed, to reach the vicinity of Richmond before they could concentrate all their troops there; that they could not get all their troops down from Manassas, and before we got there."

## Note 24.—Page 14.

*"Col. Lecompte's statement of numbers does not differ very much from one laid before a council of war, by Gen. McClellan, on the 2d of March."*

Since writing the above, I have found a memorandum taken at the time by me, which shows that even Col. Lecompte's statement *does* differ " very much" as to an important portion of the rebel forces, from " one laid before a council of war." The council was instituted as follows :

*Memorandum.* — " Generals Barnard, McDowell, Heintzelman, and Hooker, to meet Gen. Marcy and Capt. Wyman" (U. S. N.), " to-morrow, 2d March, to propose and prepare the details of a plan for opening the lower Potomac on the following basis, &c., &c."

(This was *after* the plan mentioned (p. 16) "for throwing Hooker's division across to carry" the rebel batteries " by assault," had been abandoned.)

A map was laid before the council, on which was marked the probable positions and numerical strength of the enemy's forces at Manassas and Centreville, and thence along the line to Dumfries. They were as follows :

| | | | | | |
|---|---|---|---|---|---|
| On the Dumfries Road and Jones' Station, all within 4½ miles of Dumfries road, between Neabsco and Powell's Creek, . . . . . . . . . | | | | 6,400 | |
| Between Dumfries, Evansport, and Shipping Point, . | | | . | 3,200 | |
| Hampton's Legion, Occoquan and Colchester, . | | | . | 4,000 | |
| | | | | | 13,600 |
| Near Wolf Run Shoals, . . . . . . | | | | 7,000 | |
| At Manassas, . . . . . . . | | | | 900 | |
| Near Manassas, . . . . . . | | | | 3,600 | |
| Union Mills, { Taylor's Brigade, . . . | | 4,000 | | | |
| { Elzey's " . . . | | 2,800—6,800 | | | |
| At other points not specified in Memorandum, . . | | | | 4,800 | |
| Road from Centreville to Blackburn's Ford (Bonham), . | | | | 4,000 | |
| At Centreville, { 8th Virginia, . . . | | 1,000 | | | |
| { 5 Companies, . . . | | 300—1,300 | | | |
| At Cub Run, { Jones' Brigade, . . . | | 2,500 | | | |
| { Tomb's " . . . | | 3,000—5,500 | | | |
| At "Stone Bridge," Stuart's Cavalry, . . . | | | | 3,000—36,900 | |
| | | | | 50,500 | |

By this estimate there were therefore at " Manassas, Centreville, Bull Run, and Upper Occoquan," 36,900 men instead of the forty seven thousand of the " Count of Paris," and the *eighty thousand* of the report of the " Chief of Secret Service," of March 8th, quoted by Gen. McClellan.

It is a noticeable fact, however, that, even by this diminished statement, there were in the immediate vicinity of the *batteries* against which " preparations were even made for throwing Hooker's division across the river to carry them by assault" (p. 50), a force of 9,600 men, and within two or three hours' march, 11,000 more.

To the total aggregate of 50,500, east of the Blue Ridge, a few thousand should be added for troops at Fredericksburg, and between that place and Dumfries.

# MILITARY AND NAVAL

## PUBLICATIONS,

FROM THE PRESS OF

# D. VAN NOSTRAND,

192 BROADWAY,

(UP STAIRS,)

## NEW YORK.

A large Stock of English, French, and American Military Works, constantly on hand.

Copies of any of these Books sent free by mail on receipt of the Catalogue price.

Van Nostrand's Publications.*

Comprising the History of the Tactics of the separate Arms, the Com-
bination of the Arms, and the minor operations of War.  By ED-
WARD DE LA BARRE DUPARCQ, Captain of Engineers, and Professor of the Military Art in the Imperial School of Saint Cyr.
Translated by Brig.-Gen. GEORGE W. CULLUM, U. S. A., Chief of
the Staff of Major-General H. W. Halleck, U. S. A.  1 vol. 8vo,
cloth.  $4.

"I read the original a few years since, and considered it the very best work I
had seen upon the subject.  Gen. Cullum's ability and familiarity with the
technical language of French military writers, are a sufficient guarantee of the cor-
rectness of his translation.
"H. W. HALLECK, Major-Gen., U. S. A."

"I have read the book with great interest, and trust that it will have a large
circulation.  It cannot fail to do good by spreading that very knowledge, the
want of which among our new, inexperienced, and untaught soldiers, has cost us
so many lives, and so much toil and treasure.
"M. C. MEIGS, Quartermaster-Gen., U. S. A."

"I have carefully read most of Gen. Cullum's translation of M. Barré Duparcq's
'Elements of Military Art and History.'  It is a plain, concise work, well suited to
our service.  Our volunteers should read and study it.  I wish it could be widely
circulated among our officers.  It would give them a comprehensive knowledge
of the different arms of the service, and invite further investigation into the profession of arms which they have adopted.  A careful study of such works will
make our officers learned and skilful, as well as wise and successful; and they
have ample time while they are campaigning to improve themselves in this regard.
S. R. CURTIS, Major-General, U. S. A."

## Ordnance and Armor.

The Principles, Particulars, Structure, Fabrication, and Results of
standard European and American Guns, Rifling, and Projectiles;
Metals and Combinations of Materials for Cannon; Detailed
Official Accounts of English and American Experiments against
Armor; Notes on Gun-Cotton, &c.  By ALEXANDER L. HOLLEY,
B. P, Author of "American and European Railway Practice,"
&c.  1 vol, 8vo, 600 pages, with 300 Illustrations, and copious
tables.  *In press.*

## Cavalry: its History, Management, and Uses in War.

By J. ROEMER, late an Officer of Cavalry in the service of the Nether-
lands.  1 vol. 8vo.  With over two hundred beautifully engraved
illustrations.  Price $5 00.

# School of the Guides.

Designed for the use of the Militia of the United States. Flexible cloth. 50 cents.

"This excellent compilation condenses into a compass of less than sixty pages all the instruction necessary for the guides, and the information being disconnected with other matters, is more readily referred to and more easily acquired."—*Louisville Journal.*

"The work is carefully got up, and is illustrated by numerous figures, which make the positions of the guides plain to the commonest understanding. Those of our sergeants who wish to be 'posted' in their duties should procure a copy."—*Sunday Mercury, Philadelphia.*

"It has received high praise, and will prove of great service in perfecting the drill of our Militia."—*N. American and U. S. Gazette, Phil.*

"This neat hand-book of the elementary movements on which the art of the tactician is based, reflects great credit on Col. LE GAL, whose reputation is deservedly high among military men. No soldier should be without the School of the Guides."—*New York Daily News.*

# Gunnery in 1858 :

A Treatise on Rifles, Cannon, and Sporting Arms. By WM. GREENER, C. E. 1 vol. 8vo, cloth. $3.

# Gunnery Catechism,

As Applied to the Service of Naval Ordnance, adapted to the latest Official Regulations, and approved by the Bureau of Ordnance, Navy Department. By J. D. BRANDT, formerly of the U. S. Navy. 1 vol., 18mo, cloth. *In press.*

BUREAU OF ORDNANCE—NAVY DEPARTMENT, }
WASHINGTON CITY, *May* 26, 1864. }

Mr J. D. BRANDT.—*Sir :* Your "Catechism of Gunnery, as Applied to the Service of Naval Ordnance," having been submitted to the examination of ordnance officers, and favorably recommended by them, is approved by this Bureau.
H. A. WISE, CHIEF OF BUREAU, *ad interim.*

# Auftrian Infantry Tactics.

Evolutions of the Line as practised by the Austrian Infantry, and adopted in 1853. Translated by Capt. C. M. WILCOX, Seventh Regiment U. S. Infantry. 1 vol. 12mo. Three large plates, cloth. $1.

"The movements of armies engaged in battle have often been compared to those of the chess-board, and we cannot doubt that there are certain principles of tactics in actual war as in that game, which may determine the result independently, in a great measure, of the personal strength and courage of the men engaged. The difference between these principles as applied in the American Army and in the Austrian, is so wide as to have suggested the translation of the work before us, which contains the whole result of the famous Field-Marshal RADETZKY's experience for twenty-five years, while in supreme command in Italy."—*New York Century.*

# Gunnery Instructions.

Simplified for the Volunteer Officers of the U. S. Navy, with hints to Executive and other Officers. By Lieut.-Commander EDWARD BARRETT, U. S. N., Instructor in Gunnery, Navy Yard, Brooklyn. Third edition, revised and enlarged. 1 vol. 12mo, cloth. $1 25.

"It is a thorough work, treating plainly on its subject, and contains also some valuable hints to executive officers. No officer in the volunteer navy should be without a copy."—*Boston Evening Traveller.*

"This work contains detailed and specific instructions on all points connected with the use and management of guns of every kind in the naval service. It has full illustrations, and many of these of the most elementary character, especially designed for the use of volunteers in the navy. The duties of executive officers and of the division officers are so clearly set forth, that 'he who runs may read' and understand. The manual exercise is explicit, and rendered simple by diagrams. Forms of watch and quarter bills are given; and at the close there is a table of ranges according to the kind and calibre of gun, the weight of the ball, and the charge of powder. A valuable little hand-book."—*Philadelphia Inquirer.*

"I have looked through Lieut. Barrett's book, and think it will be very valuable to the volunteer officers who are now in the naval service.

"C. R. P. RODGERS,
*Commanding U. S. Steam Frigate Wabash.*"

# The "C. S. A." and the Battle of Bull Run.

(A Letter to an English Friend.) By J. G. BARNARD, Major of Engineers, U. S. A., Brigadier-General, and Chief Engineer, Army of the Potomac. With five maps. 1 vol. 8vo, cloth. $1 50.

"This book was begun by the author as a letter to a friend in England, but as he proceeded and his MSS. increased in magnitude, he changed his original plan, and the book is the result. General Barnard gives by far the best, most comprehensible and complete account of the Battle of Bull Run we have seen. It is illustrated by some beautifully drawn maps, prepared for the War Department by the topographical engineers. He demonstrates to a certainty that but for the causeless panic the day might not have been lost. The author writes with vigor and earnestness, and has contributed one of the most valuable records yet published of the history of the war."—*Boston Commercial Bulletin.*

# Models of Fortifications.

Vauban's First System—One Front and two Bastions; Scale, 20 yards to an inch. The Modern System—One Front; Scale, 20 yards to an inch. Field-Works—The Square Redoubt; Scale, 5 yards to an inch. Mr. Kimber's three volumes, viz.: Vauban's First System, The Modern System, and Field-Works, will accompany the Models. Price for the Set of Three, with books, $75.

# Hand-Book of Artillery,

For the Service of the United States Army and Militia. New and revised edition. By Maj. Joseph Roberts, U. S. A. 1 vol. 18mo, cloth, New and enlarged edition. $1 00.

"A complete catechism of gun practice, covering the whole ground of this branch of military science, and adapted to militia and volunteer drill, as well as to the regular army. It has the merit of precise detail, even to the technical names of all parts of a gun, and how the smallest operations connected with its use can be best performed. It has evidently been prepared with great care, and with strict scientific accuracy. By the recommendation of a committee appointed by the commanding officer of the Artillery School at Fort Monroe, Va., it has been substituted for 'Burns' Questions and Answers,' an English work which has heretofore been the text-book of instruction in this country." —*New York Century.*

# New Infantry Tactics,

For the Instruction, Exercise, and Manœuvres of the Soldier, a Company, Line of Skirmishers, Battalion, Brigade, or Corps d'Armée. By Brig.-Gen. Silas Casey, U. S. A. 3 vols. 24mo. Half roan, lithographed plates. $2.50.

Vol. I.—School of the Soldier; School of the Company; Instruction for Skirmishers.

Vol. II.—School of the Battalion.

Vol. III.—Evolutions of a Brigade; Evolutions of a Corps d'Armée.

The manuscript of this new system of Infantry Tactics was carefully examined by General McClellan, and met with his unqualified approval, which he has since manifested by authorizing General Casey to adopt it for his entire division. The author has retained much that is valuable contained in the systems of Scott and Hardee, but has made many important changes and additions which experience and the exigencies of the service require. General Casey's reputation as an accomplished soldier and skilful tactician is a guarantee that the work he has undertaken has been thoroughly performed.

"These volumes are based on the French *ordonnances* of 1831 and 1845 for the manœuvres of heavy infantry and *chasseurs à pied;* both of these systems have been in use in our service for some years, the former having been translated by Gen. Scott, and the latter by Col. Hardee. After the introduction of the latter drill in our service, in connection with Gen. Scott's Tactics, there arose the necessity of a uniform system for the manœuvres of all the infantry arm of the service. These volumes are the result of the author's endeavor to communicate the instruction, now used and adopted in the army, to achieve this result."—*Boston Journal.*

"Based on the best precedents, adapted to the novel requirements of the art of war, and very full in its instructions, Casey's Tactics will be received as the most useful and most comprehensive work of its kind in our language. From the drill and discipline of the individual soldier, or through all the various combinations, to the manœuvres of a brigade and the evolutions of a Corps D'Armée, the student is advanced by a clear method and steady progress. Numerous cuts, plans, and diagrams illustrate positions and movements, and demonstrate to the eye the exact working out of the individual position, brigading, order of battle, &c., &c. The work is a model of publishing success, being in three neat pocket volumes."—*New Yorker.*

# Rifles and Rifle Practice.

An Elementary Treatise on the Theory of Rifle Firing; explaining the causes of Inaccuracy of Fire and the manner of correcting it; with descriptions of the Infantry Rifles of Europe and the United States, their Balls and Cartridges. By Capt. C. M. WILCOX, U. S. A. New edition, with engravings and cuts. Green cloth. $1.75.

"Although eminently a scientific work, special care seems to have been taken to avoid the use of technical terms, and to make the whole subject readily comprehensible to the practical enquirer. It was designed chiefly for the use of Volunteers and Militia; but the War Department has evinced its approval of its merits by ordering from the publisher one thousand copies, for the use of the United States Army."—*Louisville Journal.*

"The book will be found intensely interesting to all who are watching the changes in the art of war arising from the introduction of the new rifled arms. We recommend to our readers to buy the book."—*Military Gazette.*

" A most valuable treatise."—*New York Herald.*

"This book is quite original in its character. That character is completeness. It renders a study of most of the works on the rifle that have been published quite unnecessary. We cordially recommend the book."—*United Service Gazette, London.*

"The work being in all its parts derived from the best sources, is of the highest authority, and will be accepted as the standard on the subject of which it treats."—*New Yorker.*

# Army Officer's Pocket Companion.

Principally designed for Staff Officers in the Field. Partly translated from the French of M. DE ROUVRE, Lieutenant-Colonel of the French Staff Corps, with Additions from Standard American, French, and English Authorities. By WM. P. CRAIGHILL, First Lieutenant U. S. Corps of Engineers, Assist. Prof. of Engineering at the U. S. Military Academy, West Point. 1 vol. 18mo. Full roan. $1.50.

"I have carefully examined Capt. CRAIGHILL's Pocket Companion. I find it one of the very best works of the kind I have ever seen. Any Army or Volunteer officer who will make himself acquainted with the contents of this little book, will seldom be ignorant of his duties in camp or field."
H. W. HALLECK,
Major-General U. S. A.

"I have carefully examined the 'Manual for Staff Officers in the Field.' It is a most invaluable work, admirable in arrangement, perspicuously written, abounding in most useful matters, and such a book as should be the constant pocket companion of every army officer, Regular and Volunteer."
G. W. CULLUM,
Brigadier-General U. S. A.
Chief of General Halleck's Staff,
Chief Engineer Department Mississippi.

"This little volume contains a large amount of indispensable information relating to officers' duties in the siege, camp, and field, and will prove to them a most valuable pocket companion. It is illustrated with plans and drawings."
—*Boston Com. Bulletin.*

# Sword-Play.

THE MILITIAMAN'S MANUAL AND SWORD-PLAY WITHOUT A MASTER.—Rapier and Broad-Sword Exercises copiously Explained and Illustrated; Small-Arm Light Infantry Drill of the United States Army; Infantry Manual of Percussion Muskets; Company Drill of the United States Cavalry. By Major M. W. BERRIMAN, engaged for the last thirty years in the practical instruction of Military Students. Second edition. 1 vol. 12mo, red cloth. $1.

"Captain Berriman has had thirty years' experience in teaching military students, and his work is written in a simple, clear, and soldierly style. It is illustrated with twelve plates, and is one of the cheapest and most complete works of the kind published in this country." —*New York World.*

"This work will be found very valuable to all persons seeking military instruction; but it recommends itself most especially to officers, and those who have to use the sword or sabre. We believe it is the only work on the use of the sword published in this country."—*New York Tablet.*

"It is a work of obvious merit and value."—*Boston Traveller.*

# Military Law and Courts Martial,

By Capt. S. V. BENET, U. S. Ordnance, Asst. Prof. of Ethics in the United States Military Academy. 1 vol. 8vo. Law sheep, $3.50.

# The Artillerift's Manual :

Compiled from various Sources, and adapted to the Service of the United States. Profusely illustrated with woodcuts and engravings on stone. Second edition, revised and corrected, with valuable additions, By Capt. JOHN GIBBON, U. S. Army. 1 vol. 8vo, half roan, $5;

This book is now considered the standard authority for that particular branch of the Service in the United States Army. The War Department, at Washington, has exhibited its thorough appreciation of the merits of this volume, the want of which has been hitherto much felt in the service, by subscribing for 700 copies.

"It is with great pleasure that we welcome the appearance of a new work on this subject, entitled 'The Artillerist's Manual,' by Capt. John Gibbon, a highly scientific and meritorious officer of artillery in our regular service. The work, an octavo volume of 500 pages, in large, clear type, appears to be well adapted to supply just what has been heretofore needed to fill the gap between the simple Manual and the more abstruse demonstrations of the science of gunnery. The whole work is profusely illustrated with woodcuts and engravings on stone, tending to give a more complete and exact idea of the various matters described in the text. The book may well be considered as a valuable and important addition to the military science of the country."—*New York Herald.*

# Siege of Bomarfund (1854).

Journals of Operations of the Artillery and Engineers. Published by permission of the Minister of War. Illustrated by maps and plans. Translated from the French by an Army Officer. 1 vol. 12mo, cloth. 75 cents.

"To military men this little volume is of special interest. It contains a translation by an officer of the United States Army, of the journal of operations by the artillery and engineers at the siege of Bomarsund in 1854, published by permission of the French Minister of War in the *Journal des Armées speciales et de l'État Major.* The account of the same successful attack, given by Sir Howard Douglas in the new edition of his work on Gunnery, is appended; and the narrative is illustrated by elaborate maps and plans."—*New York Paper.*

# Lefsons and Practical Notes on Steam,

The Steam-Engine, Propellers, &c., &c., for Young Marine Engineers, Students, and others. By the late W. R. KING, U. S. N. Revised by Chief-Engineer J. W KING, U. S. Navy. Fifth edition, enlarged. 8vo, cloth. $2.00

"This is the second edition of a valuable work of the late W. R. KING, U. S. N. It contains lessons and practical notes on Steam and the Steam-Engine, Propellers, &c. It is calculated to be of great use to young marine engineers, students, and others. The text is illustrated and explained by numerous diagrams and representations of machinery. This new edition has been revised and enlarged by Chief Engineer J. W. KING, U. S. N., brother to the deceased author of the work."—*Boston Daily Advertiser.*

"This is one of the best, because eminently plain and practical, treatises on the Steam-Engine ever published."—*Philadelphia Press.*

"Its re-publication at this time, when so many young men are entering the service as naval engineers, is most opportune. Each of them ought to have a copy."—*Philadelphia Evening Bulletin.*

# Manual of Internal Rules and Regulations for Men-of-War.

By Commodore U. P. LEVY, U. S. N., late Flag-officer commanding U. S. Naval Force in the Mediterranean, &c. Flexible blue cloth. Second edition, revised and enlarged. 50 cents.

"Among the professional publications for wh'ch we are indebted to the war, we willingly give a prominent place to this useful little Manual of Rules and Regulations to be observed on board of ships of war. Its authorship is a sufficient guarantee for its accuracy and practical value; and as a guide to young officers in providing for the discipline, police, and sanitary government of the vessels under their command, we know of nothing superior."—*N. Y. Herald.*

"Should be in the hands of every Naval officer, of whatever grade, and will not come amiss to any intelligent mariner."—*Boston Traveller.*

"A work which will prove of great utility, in both the Naval service and the mercantile marine."—*Baltimore American.*

# Evolutions of Field Batteries of Artillery.

Translated from the French, and arranged for the Army and Militia
of the United States. By Gen. ROBERT ANDERSON, U. S. Army.
Published by order of the War Department. 1 vol. cloth, 32
plates. $1.

WAR DEPARTMENT, *Nov. 2d,* 1859.

The System of "Evolutions of Field Batteries," translated from the French,
and arranged for the service of the United States, by Major Robert Anderson,
of the 1st Regiment of Artillery, having been approved by the President, is
published for the information and government of the army.

All Evolutions of Field Batteries not embraced in this system are prohibited,
and those herein prescribed will be strictly observed.

J. B. FLOYD, *Secretary of War.*

"This system having been adopted by the War Department, is to the artillerist what Hardee's Tactics is to the infantry soldier; the want of a work like
this has been seriously felt, and will be eagerly welcomed."—*Louisville Journal.*

# Hiftory of the United States Naval Academy

With Biographical Sketches, and the names of all the Superintendents,
Professors and Graduates, to which is added a Record of some
of the earliest Votes by Congress, of Thanks, Medals and Swords
to Naval Officers. By EDWARD CHAUNCEY MARSHALL, A. M.,
formerly Instructor in Captain Kinsley's Military School at West
Point, Assistant Professor in the N. Y. University, etc. $1.

# Ordnance and Gunnery.

A Course of Instruction in Ordnance and Gunnery. Compiled for
the Use of the Cadets of the United States Military Academy.
By Captain J. G. BENTON, Ordnance Department U. S. A., late
Instructor of Ordnance and the Science of Gunnery, U. S. Military Academy, West Point, and First Assistant to the Chief
of Ordnance, U. S. A. Second edition, revised and enlarged.
1 vol. 8vo, half morocco, $5.

Capt. Benton has carefully revised and corrected this valuable work on Ordnance and Gunnery, the first edition of which was published only about a year
ago. The many important improvements introduced in this branch of the service
have rendered such a revision necessary. The present edition will be invaluable, not only to the student, but as a standard book of reference on the subject
of which it treats.

# Scott's Military Dictionary.

Comprising Technical Definitions; Information on Raising and Keeping Troops; Actual Service, including makeshifts and improved materiel, and Law, Government, Regulation, and Administration relating to Land Forces. By Colonel H. L. Scott, Inspector-General U. S. A. 1 vol., large octavo, fully illustrated, half morocco. $6.

"It is a complete Encyclopædia of Military Science."—*Philadelphia Evening Bulletin.*

"We cannot speak too much in legitimate praise of this work."—*National Intelligencer.*

"It should be made a Text-book for the study of every Volunteer."—*Harper's Magazine.*

"We cordially commend it to public favor."—*Washington Globe.*

"This comprehensive and skilfully prepared work supplies a want that has long been felt, and will be peculiarly valuable at this time as a book of reference."—*Boston Commercial Bulletin.*

"The Military Dictionary is splendidly got up in every way, and reflects credit on the publisher. The officers of every company in the service should possess it."—*N. Y. Tablet.*

"The work is more properly a Military Encyclopædia, and is profusely illustrated with engravings. It appears to contain every thing that can be wanted in the shape of information by officers of all grades."—*Philadelphia North American.*

"This book is really an Encyclopædia, both elementary and technical, and as such occupies a gap in military literature which has long been most inconveniently vacant. This book meets a present popular want, and will be secured not only by those embarking in the profession but by a great number of civilians, who are determined to follow the descriptions and to understand the philosophy of the various movements of the campaign. Indeed, no tolerably good library would be complete without the work."—*New York Times.*

"The work has evidently been compiled from a careful consultation of the best authorities, enriched with the results of the experience and personal knowledge of the author."—*N. Y. Daily Tribune.*

"Works like the present are invaluable. The officers of our Volunteer service would all do well to possess themselves of the volume."—*N. Y. Herald.*

# New Bayonet Exercise.

A New Manual of the Bayonet, for the Army and Militia of the United States. By Colonel J. C. Kelton, U. S. A. With thirty beautifully-engraved plates. Red cloth. $1.75.

This Manual was prepared for the use of the Corps of Cadets, and has been introduced at the Military Academy with satisfactory results. It is simply the theory of the attack and defence of the sword applied to the bayonet, on the authority of men skilled in the use of arms.

The Manual contains practical lessons in Fencing, and prescribes the defence against Cavalry and the manner of conducting a contest with a Swordsman.

"This work merits a favorable reception at the hands of all military men. It contains all the instruction necessary to enable an officer to drill his men in the use of this weapon. The introduction of the Sabre Bayonet in our Army renders a knowledge of the exercise more imperative."—*New York Times.*

CPSIA information can be obtained
at www.ICGtesting.com
Printed in the USA
BVHW070111140421
604815BV00008B/550